THE MINUTES
A Guide for Company Secretaries and Managers

To
my daughter
HARRIET
who never seems to have a minute for anything

The Minutes

A Guide for Company
Secretaries and Managers

SIMON MORT

Gower

Published by
Gower Publishing Company Limited
Gower House
Croft Road
Aldershot
Hants GU11 3HR
England

Gower Publishing Company
Old Post Road
Brookfield
Vermont 05036
USA

British Library Cataloguing in Publication Data
Mort, Simon
  The minutes: a guide for company secretaries.
  1. Organizations. Meetings. Minutes
  I. Title
  657.77

Library of Congress Cataloguing-in-Publication Data
Mort, Simon
  The minutes: a guide for company secretaries and managers / Simon Mort.
    p. cm.
  Includes bibliographical references (p.   ) and index.
  1. Meetings—Handbooks, manuals, etc. ". Corporate minutes–
–Handbooks, manuals, etc. I. Title.
HF5734.5.M67 1991
651.7'7—dc20
                                                        90–24219
                                                        CIP

ISBN 0566 02708 9

Printed in England by Clays Ltd, St Ives plc

Contents

List of figures

Preface

To many people minutes are threatening. To those who take them, the responsibility for keeping an adequate record of the deliberations and the strong feelings frequently expressed is a daunting one. To those who read them, minutes are often felt to be a superficial and insufficient account of their personal contribution. A senior manager from one of the utility industries commented: 'We don't call them minutes. We call them notes. We get more cooperation that way.'

This book seeks to provide guidance for everyone who is faced with the problems of taking such minutes. Most of the examples are from commercial contexts, but the lessons drawn from them should easily be applicable to a wide variety of environments. Minutes are needed for the cricket club, the pensioners' society, the party political branch and the parochial church council. Although many of the illustrations may be more complex than would apply to these kinds of minutes, the underlying message should apply to them all.

Thanks are due to many people who have encouraged me to write the book, in particular Richard Malthouse, Michael Tolond and Gordon Willimont of Fisons Pharmaceuticals. It was felt by these and other people that there was no simple textbook to help new minute-takers with layout, content or style. The following pages are intended to respond to that encouragement and to fill the void.

As with earlier requests to publish material which is private and internal to particular companies and organizations, I have been astonished by the generosity of those who have given permission for its release. In particular I am delighted to record grateful thanks to:

Roger Wheywell	(Bayer UK Limited)
Fergus Robertson	(British Institute of Management)
Bernard Simpson	(British Red Cross Society)
Liz Bryant	(Centre for British Teachers Limited)
Roger Dudman	(Chartered Association for Certified Accountants)
Christopher Curtis	(Council for Small Industries in Rural Areas)
Phil Gibson	(Dearborn Chemicals Ltd)
Pamela Guiles	(Flight Refuelling Limited)
Stephen Rose	(Glaxo Pharmaceuticals)
J. D. Rimington	(Health and Safety Executive)
Saeed Abu Lugoud	(Joint Operations)
B. R. Simister	(London Brick Company Limited)
John Hearn	(London Underground Limited)
M. J. Thompson	(Northern Telecom Europe Limited)
Libby Glare-Williams	(Shanks & McEwan [Southern] Limited)
Gordon Fawcett	(States of Jersey)

John Raine   (Tyne and Wear Passenger Transport
                              Executive)
Sheena MacDonald   (Willis Faber & Dumas)

Discussion with Joan Bailey of the Cabinet Office has been especially
valuable. Several chapters make quite extensive reference to Cabinet
minutes (known as conclusions). This is because their techniques and
history demonstrate so many of the problems, demands and challenges
inherent in minutes: extreme conciseness, wide-ranging subject matter,
diverse busy readerships, prejudice and strong feelings, confidentiality
and integrity. The particular hallmarks of Cabinet minutes are conciseness and objectivity. Conciseness, always a desirable feature of
written communications, is vital in minutes prepared for Ministers,
who may have to read them in great haste in the back of the car or
some other inconvenient place.

The examples from Cabinet minutes are necessarily taken from 30
years ago, because of the law of disclosure. However, all the points
drawn from them are still valid in current Cabinet Office practice.

I am very grateful to Ken Brooks of Linnells, the Oxford solicitors,
for his advice on the legal status of minutes. Much evidence of his
wise guidance is to be found in Appendix II.

Particular thanks are due to Margaret Ferré of Her Majesty's Stationery Office for her advice over the Committee of Public Accounts
proceedings at Figure 5.1.

Finally, none of this would have happened without the confidence,
support and understanding of Malcolm Stern of Gower. Nor would
the words have seen print without the efforts of Janey Moore who
produced the typescript and carried out some exceptionally tedious
research tasks, or Janice Coventry who typed all the correspondence
and kept giving me firm but courteous reminders that it was high
time the book was finished.

                                                            Simon Mort

1 THE NATURE OF MINUTES

Minutes constitute a record which serves four purposes:

- They must remind participants of what happened at the last meeting.
- They must provide a basis for discussion of matters arising.
- They must be sufficiently complete for those who were not present at the meeting to understand what took place.
- They must provide a permanent record.

These functions represent the dominant themes of this book. The third in particular needs to be stressed. Minutes are not just an *aide-mémoire* to jog the memories of those who were there. They must provide a comprehensive but concise guide for those who were not present, through holiday, sickness or other duties, as well as for those who cannot clearly remember the details of the occasion. A comment on the meaning and range of the term *minutes* is important in defining the scope and range of this book.

Minutes suggest a conventional and formal meeting with an appointed chairman and secretary. Equally relevant are impromptu meetings and their related documents which are often called *records of meetings*. These will frequently be less formal documents compiled by a junior person present; they may not refer directly to an agenda, but in other respects should follow the conventions and principles of minutes.

Action Notes is an increasingly fashionable term. Such a title places a psychological emphasis on decisions and action to be taken. However, for the action points to be meaningful, it is usually necessary to include a fair amount of detail concerning their background and context.

Visit Reports frequently and quite properly take a form similar to that of minutes. As in a more structured meeting, a group of people with a common purpose come together to investigate a number of points and record their findings. This is illustrated by the visit by Flight Refuelling Limited whose aim was to test a production batch:

```
FLIGHT REFUELLING LIMITED      PRODUCTION CONTROL DEPARTMENT

Our ref:  PC/GH/RAH/2069

                           VISIT REPORT

Company visited            Robert Jenkins Limited

Date visited               24th January 1986

Personnel present          Mr Hardy     Works Manager RJSL

                           Mr Madner    Assistant Works Manager RJSL

                           Mr Bottom    FRL

                           Mr Owen      FRL

                           Mr Haywood   FRL
```

All these forms serve a similar purpose: to record discussions, and sometimes events, as concisely as possible. Unlike a report, a set of minutes need not stand on its own. It is part of a chain and each minute may depend on earlier minutes to convey the whole story.

Variations between meeting proceedings and minutes

The ethics of minutes are important: the chairman's role is discussed in Chapter 8, and the legal aspects in Appendix II.

After the meeting there will often be a temptation to change and amend the first draft of the minutes. Sometimes a chairman completely rewrites the minutes, with scant regard to the secretary's first draft. This is highly irregular and unprincipled. There are very few occasions in which the minutes should deliberately deviate from a true, accurate and balanced account of the meeting. Such exceptions are:

- Cases of exceptional discretion or confidentiality. (In such cases a description may legitimately be omitted from the minutes.)
- Matters of very local or esoteric importance only. (Here the individual concerned may make a personal note.)
- Highly generalized minutes which are only an indication of progress. In this case even the loosest record of the discussion is irrelevant.
- Very exceptionally, specific detail which has come to light after the meeting.

One of the most instructive set of guidelines on the purpose and general philosophy of minutes is that circulated by the current (1990) Director-General of the Health & Safety Executive:

Minutes

4. When writing minutes, do not attribute statements to particular people or groups unless this is essential; either because no one else agreed or because a particular authority belongs to the originator. Say "In further discussion, the following points were made (a), (b), (c) etc".

5. Never include verbiage such as "Opening the meeting, the chairman said ..." or "Welcoming Mr X ... etc". What does it add?

6. Use your discretion. Never put nonsense into someone's mouth, even if he did talk nonsense. In the extreme case, omit the point. In a less extreme case, expand that part of what was said that did make sense. Minutes are properly NOT a record of what took place, but of how agreement was reached or disagreement arose; usually agreement is founded on the sense that was talked.

Problems

Many minute-takers find their duties irritating. They are not challenging in that they do not demand original thought. They are tedious in that they merely involve reprocessing other people's thoughts and ideas. They are politically sensitive in that the minute-writers have a responsibility to represent other people's feelings more concisely than they were originally expressed but without distorting their ideas. The most common dilemmas are:

- How to lay the minutes out;
- How much information to put in;
- What style/tone to adopt.

These problems will be addressed in the following pages.

The politics of minutes

The meeting relies on the secretary to make the record. Others present will undoubtedly take rough notes, which will certainly be selective and at times may contradict those of the secretary. The latter's version will be the definitive record and must reflect that responsibility in its accuracy.

There is a need to satisfy everyone at the meeting. Contributors will have argued at length and in detail. A shorter record of the meeting is bound to reduce and simplify these views. Individuals will often consider that issues about which they feel strongly should be expressed at greater length and more forcefully in the minutes.

Summary

Minutes are partly reminder, partly agenda for the next meeting, partly a brief for those absent and partly permanent record. They must be sufficiently complete to be understood by those who were not present.

The principles of minutes apply also to visit reports and to informal notes of meetings.

The Secretary's record of a meeting must be definitive. Tact and force of personality may often be required to counter less careful records kept by participants.

2 THE IMPORTANCE OF MINUTES

Management time is scarce and thus a valuable commodity. Meetings should only be convened when they are absolutely necessary; that is, when important issues need to be discussed. Minutes are the only permanent record of the event. It is therefore essential that they:

● Be concise;
● Be accurate and complete;
● Be expressed in a form that satisfies all the participants, and
● Convey the tone of the meeting.

Successfully balancing all these aspects within a limited space is extremely difficult; it is this which represents the skill of writing minutes.

Conciseness

In the course of a meeting a great deal will be said which has no place in the minutes. There will be irrelevance, illustrations to endorse a point and a great deal of repetition. Much repetition is both inevitable and excusable. During the course of even the briefest meeting, attention is bound to wander. There will be distractions. People will go in and out of the room. Traffic and other noises from outside are likely to obscure comments.

Some participants will deliberately distract the meeting with red herrings. Wits will seek to entertain it with humour or ribaldry which, even if relevant, is totally inappropriate for a permanent record. Some will use the occasion to show off their knowledge of the subject-matter. Lee Iacocca was a senior employee of Henry Ford. He turned meetings into what Ford's biographers Collier and Horowitz called 'a showcase of his own expertise . . . aware of its lingo and intricacies' in a way that Ford was not. As a result Ford would come out of the meeting and ask, 'What the hell was Lee talking about? What was the point of all that?'[1] This is a slightly crude shorthand form of the questions the secretary has to ask him/herself in order to pick out what is important from all the verbiage.

An agenda item may be discussed for 40 or 45 minutes. When all this is reduced to the minuted form it will probably take up no more than ten lines of typescript. This exchange from the oral evidence of the Welsh Development Agency to the Wilson Committee illustrates the point:[2]

> *Sir David Orr:* What calibre of people have been coming along to you? Are they all entrepreneurs who have started young in setting up their own business? Are they people who have had experience in larger companies who now want to branch out on their own? What sort of people are coming along?
> *Mr Loveland:* I think there is a fair mix, but most of them are entrepreneurs who have started up on their own at various times of life and are that peculiar breed of small to medium sized businessmen. If I may expand on that, they are more often than not very expert in their field. Equally, more often than not they are lacking generally in commercial expertise. They may be super engineers, they may be super product innovators, they may have a particular knowledge of a particular market. But in the totality of business in one element or more they are lacking.

The whole of this might be consolidated in minutes as:

> All sorts of people sought help, especially from small or medium businesses, but most lacked commercial expertise.

The account must be more complete than would be considered sufficient for a personal note or a diary entry. Consider this seemingly complete note from J. Paul Getty's diary:[3]

> Jerry Williams brought us up to date on North Sea developments and then we considered the budget, much increased due to inflation.

The note is doubtless admirable as an *aide-mémoire* but it will not suffice as a minute. Several questions remain unanswered: What did Williams say about the North Sea? What aspects of the budget were covered? What figures were forthcoming? How great was the increase due to inflation? Did this matter? Indeed did Jerry Williams' comments lead to any call for action?

This distinction between an *aide-mémoire* and a minute being crucial, it is elaborated further hereafter.

Accuracy and completeness

Conciseness may be just a concession to the reader's convenience. It takes more effort and more time to read something than it does to listen to it. Accuracy relates more to the integrity of the record. Inaccuracy is sometimes the result of the minute-taker's incompetence, inexperience or lack of the relevant skills. Sometimes the cause is more sinister.

Full and complete notes taken at the time have an advantage over those written up afterwards from memory. In the preface to her personal account of the second Wilson administration, Dame Barbara Castle wrote:

> Because I do shorthand, and because I laboured hard at some physical cost to keep as full a record as possible, I believe my diaries will help to produce a rounded history of Harold Wilson's period of government.[4]

Judith Hart endorsed the greater accuracy of the Castle accounts compared with those of Richard Crossman, who lacked shorthand skills.[5]

Significantly, the importance of notes made at the time has been endorsed in court recently. While the judgement related to a file note of a conversation, its principle could certainly be applied to minutes. In *Abdulhamid Jamal Shamji and others* v. *Johnson Matthey Bankers Limited and others* (1986), one of many cases arising from the Johnson Matthey débâcle of the mid-1980s, it was held not only that a file note was good evidence of a discussion, but also that a contemporaneous note was better than one made after the event.

A subsequent part of the findings of the County NatWest inquiry depended on two meetings on 29 September 1987. The first was a meeting of the Bank's UK Business Committee. It was minuted, in part, in the following terms:[6]

> Since the end of the half year the Department has been advising Blue Arrow on its successful acquisition of Manpower which involved the largest rights issue ever seen in the UK. The Chairman commented that the Audit Committee had noted this transaction and wondered whether this was an appropriate risk for the Group to be taking. Mr Cohen replied that he was totally confident with the transaction which many believed would be seen as one of the corporate highlights of 1987 within the City. The transaction has

already raised the stature of County NatWest with a number of major corporate groups.

The department continues to be fully occupied and it is hoped that the results for the full year will show record profits.

This indicated that all was well with the rights issue. Shortly afterwards, another meeting was held, attended by several of the members of the UK Business Committee. Here a franker view emerged, but apparently no record was kept for reasons of confidentiality.

Political acceptability

Completeness is not necessarily a matter of length. The way in which the points are made must be acceptable to everyone at the meeting as a sound record of what took place. Richard Crossman, who served in Harold Wilson's first government, is outspoken and cynical on this subject. He writes in his diary that Cabinet minutes 'do not pretend to be an account of what actually takes place in the Cabinet'.[7]

He suggested that similar dishonesty exists in the minutes of Cabinet Committees: 'Normally, what they record is not what was actually said but a summary of the official brief which the Minister brought with him, the official papers on the original policy and the official conclusions.'

The implications of this kind of pre-ordained minuting are serious. They allow no scope for inclusion of comments which have arisen during the meeting and suggest that the meeting has been fixed.

Representation of the tone

There may be acrimony at a meeting and strong feelings expressed. Whereas an abusive argument cannot be recorded blow-by-blow, the tone of the confrontation should be represented.

An occasion when the normally even-tempered Charles Clore lost his temper and violently ejected the union secretary of the Musicians' Union from a meeting was an instance when representation of tone would have been critical. He was subsequently fined £8-8-0 (£8.40) for threatening behaviour, describing it subsequently as 'the best spent money in my life'.[8]

Not surprisingly, Crossman had a comment to make on this aspect too: 'The minutes never describe the real struggle which took place. That struggle is only abstracted in the form of "in the course of discussion the following points were made . . .". And in this summary the name of the Minister who made the point is rarely mentioned.'[9] Ironically, with a body such as the Cabinet speaking – at least theoretically – with one voice and having corporate responsibility, this more general overview can be appropriate.

Summary

Minutes have to tell the story long after the participants have moved on elsewhere. They must record the complete event concisely and with as much attention to the sentiments of the participants as possible. In a limited space, this is not easy. In reaching this compromise lies the skill of minute-taking.

Notes and references

1. Peter Collier and David Horowitz, *The Fords*, London: Collins, 1988.
2. *The Committee to Review the Functioning of Financial Institutions*, London: HMSO, 28 February 1978, 16.
3. J Paul Getty, *As I see It*, London: W.H. Allen, 1976.
4. Barbara Castle, *The Castle Diaries* [1974-6] London: Weidenfeld and Nicolson, 1980.
5. *New Statesman*, 3 October 1980.
6. *County NatWest Limited, County NatWest Securities Limited: Investigations under Section 432(2) of the Companies Act 1985*, report by Michael Crystal QC and David Lane Spence, CA, London: HMSO, 1989.
7. *The Crossman Diaries*, introduced and edited by Anthony Howard, London: Magnum Books, 1979.
8. David Clutterbuck and Marion Devine, *Clore: The Man and his Millions*, London: Weidenfeld and Nicolson, 1987.
9. *The Crossman Diaries*.

3 THE SUPERSCRIPTION

An essential preliminary to the body of the minutes is the heading. Its seemingly tedious details are essential, for several important reasons: they identify the subject of the meeting for easy reference (just as a report title itemizes the subject of the report); they distinguish the reports from other sets of minutes; they provide a record of those associated with the decisions and are a courtesy to those present.

In broad terms, the superscription of a set of minutes is likely to consist of the following components:

- The title of the company or organization;
- The title of the minutes, including the date;
- A list of those present, and
- Lists of those not present.

There are, of course, many logical and sensible variations, as the following illustrations will show.

Title of the company

The title of the company is generally shown at the top of the sheet, as a form of rudimentary identification for the benefit of those who receive numerous sets of minutes from various sources. It will often include the name of the department or committee, as follows:

```
                    PHARMACEUTICAL DIVISION
        REVISION OF RAW AND PACKAGING MATERIALS CONTROL
```

```
              BRITISH RED CROSS SOCIETY

                  9 Grosvenor Crescent
                  London SW1X 7EJ
```

Title of the minutes, including date

Various permutations of this information can exist. The minimum will be (a) the title of the meeting and (b) its date, as in:

```
PHARMACEUTICAL PRODUCTION MANAGERS/SHOP STEWARDS
    MEETING, HELD ON WEDNESDAY, 10 AUGUST 1983
```

Some circumstances may call for more detail, notably the time of the meeting and the room in which it was held, as in this example from Willis Faber & Dumas:

```
              SYSTEMS STAFF COMMITTEE

Minutes of Meeting held on Thursday 13 November 1986
     in Conference Room 6, Friars Street, at 2.30pm
```

In some cases a formal letter-head will be used and may include a security classification, as with the British Institute of Management minutes (Figure 3.1) which are graded CONFIDENTIAL.

BIM **Board of Directors**

CONFIDENTIAL

BIMF(82)M/4
12.11.82

FOURTH (1982) MEETING OF THE BOARD OF DIRECTORS
OF BIM FOUNDATION

held on Friday 12 November 1982 at 10.30 am
Britannia Suite Drury Lane Hotel Drury Lane WC2

Figure 3.1 British Institute of Management board minutes heading

If the time at which the meeting closed is to be shown, the time at which it opened must, of course, be shown as well. In massive establishments such as government ministries, the room in which the meeting took place is usually included as this can help to jog the memories of those burdened with several meetings in one day.

46th Conclusions

CABINET

CONCLUSIONS of a Meeting of the Cabinet held at 10 Downing Street, S.W.1 on Wednesday 4th June 1985, at 11 am

---

Cabinet minutes (or conclusions as they are known) are also given a specific number, as shown at the top left of the above example. Likewise a Red Cross committee meeting may include a relevant identifying number.

UNIFORM WORKING PARTY NO 14

MINUTES OF THE FOURTEENTH MEETING OF THE UNIFORM WORKING PARTY HELD ON THURSDAY 5th NOVEMBER 1981, AT 9 GROSVENOR CRESCENT AT 11.00 AM

List of those present

It is at this seemingly straightforward stage that numerous variations present themselves. A simple list would look like the following from Systems Division of Willis Faber & Dumas:

Present	S M C MacDonald (Chairman)
	R Marsh (Minutes)
	S Flory
	J Hicks
	I Boreham
CC	D H Smith
	D Podd

This demonstrates the generally accepted principles that:

- The chairman comes first;
- The secretary comes second or last, and
- Copy addressees (if any) are shown last of all.

If there is no specific and undisputed order, participants should be listed alphabetically. Since few situations exist in which the hierarchy is entirely undisputed and incontrovertible, alphabetical order will be the norm. However, there are some environments in which different levels can safely be identified and used. Grades in the civil service, ranks in the armed services or the police, partners/managers/assistant managers and junior staff in a firm of chartered accountants, board members/directors/officers in the Arts Council or numbered grades in, say, Ford Motor Company are examples of such explicitly stratified organizations where this kind of layering may be reflected in the list of attenders. Within such a list, of course, members of the same level are shown in alphabetical order.

Sometimes it will be helpful to show the department, union or appointment of those present, as in this illustration from Tyne and Wear Passenger Transport Executive.

```
PRESENT FOR THE EXECUTIVE

Mr D. P. C. Fletcher        (Director General - Chairman)
Mr D. F. Howard             (Director of Engineering)
Mr R. Walker                (Director of Finance)
Mr G. E. Hutchinson         (Director of Integrated Operations)
Mr P. J. Smith              (County Treasurer)

PRESENT FOR THE COMPANIES

Mr K. Holmes                (General Manager - United)
Mr M. S. A. Ballinger       (General Manager - Northern)
Mr P. J. Harmer             (Northern Regional Executive - NBC)

IN ATTENDANCE

Mr G. Brindle               (Assistant County Clerk)
Mr M. Allen                 (Associate Director Personnel - PTE)
Miss J. M. Freeman          (Secretary - PTE)
```

Cabinet minutes also show those in attendance, including ministers who are not Cabinet members.

The expression '(Deputizing)' sometimes appears in brackets after an individual's name as an oblique courtesy to the representative who normally presides. It may therefore have political value, but is generally unnecessary.

Often it will be desirable to segregate those who were attending in a non-participative role, as observers or expert advisers, as shown in the last block of the Tyne and Wear illustration above. This practice ensures that such people cannot be held responsible for the decisions of the meeting.

Special welcomes are sometimes desirable for visitors or a new member of staff.

The meeting welcomed by Mr O. Goldsmith, Sales Training Manager, and, newly appointed, Northern District Consultant, Mr R. Sheridan.

The names of Messrs Goldsmith and Sheridan would also appear in the list of those present.

Here is a complete attendance list from the Kuwait company Joint Operations.

PRESENT:

Mr. I. I. Salmeen	Head of Administration (Chairman)
Mr. S. Abu-Lugoud	Manager JOINT OPERATION
Mr. A. A. Al-Khabbaz	Supdt. General Services
Mr. A. Samara	Supdt. Materials
Mr. S. Gerges	Supdt. Contracts Admin.
Mr. M. N. A/Qader	Supdt. Personnel & Training
Mr. H. Agel	Supvr. (Production, Repr. of Operation Dept.)
Mr. Mabrouk	Accountant, System & Procedures
Mr. J. Anis	Supvr. Const. & Mtce. (SSL)
Mr. A. Al-Haj	Supvr. Fire & Safety
Mr. Z. Al-Zamel	Asst. Safety Officer
Mr. Y. Abdulla	Asst. Safety Officer
Mr. A. Bakes	Supvr. Transport & Plant
Mr M. Anis	Supvr. General Services (Secretary)

It illustrates a number of useful points. Regardless of seniority, the chairman appears first and the secretary last. In fact, Mr Abu-Lugoud is the head of the company (his title 'Manager' is misleading) but appears second as he was not chairing the meeting. The list also shows the importance of showing full titles when many of them are similar.

The secretariat members responsible for taking Cabinet minutes are recorded at the foot of the cover-sheet on which the attendance is shown.

```
                    Secretariat:

                Mr B.S.T.J. TREND
                Mr J.S. ORME
                Mr G.H. BAKER
```

Those not present

Those who have submitted apologies, either by letter beforehand or by sending a message with someone who has turned up, must be listed after those present. It is often irrelevant to put the name of the body which they represent, since they have not actually represented them. They can probably best be listed in one or more long horizontal lines:

```
Apologies were received from J. Keats, P. Shelley,
        C. Dickens, E. Brontë, J. Austen.
```

In this way they will appear less significant than those who were present, either in the role of participants or of observers.

Some organizations, such as church councils, clubs, societies and political associations, have the understandable but unfelicitous custom of naming those who sent apologies individually, but describing those who were there *en masse*, as follows:

```
Present:                   Chairman, Secretary, Treasurer
                           plus 47 other members

Apologies were received from Cllr Mrs Woolf, O. Wilde, C. Dickens.
```

It is easy to see how this position is reached. The secretary wishes to acknowledge the courtesy of those who sent apologies, but finds the list of those present too extensive to include. Yet the result is rather an illogical imbalance whereby people who were not there are given more prominence than those who were. To list all of them at the top of the minutes would often run on to a second page and be absurd. Perhaps in such cases where the attendance list is massive, it could legitimately be moved to an appendix. Reference to this fact would, of course, be made at the head of the minutes.

Just as important as the record of those who were absent for the whole time is the note of those who popped in and out. There are four ways of doing this:

1. Making a note in the body of the minutes, like a stage direction in a play:

```
        (Mr W. Wordsworth left at this point.)
```

This has the disadvantage that anyone interested in discovering whether Wordsworth was present when some, perhaps outrageous, decision was taken has to hunt through the whole set of minutes to elicit this information.

2. Putting the unhappy phrase 'part-time' against Mr Wordsworth's name in the list of those present, which the reader can see immediately in their perusal of the minutes. However such a scheme has two important drawbacks. It may give the impression that Wordsworth is not a full-time employee or, more jocularly, that he failed to concentrate during the meeting. More significantly, it does not specify at what point he went away (or came in), so that the reader is back at square one, not knowing what items to associate with him.

3. Indicating the time at which the member left, as:

```
            Ms G. Eliot (left at 3.20)
```

This is almost useless. It shows that she was not there for the whole meeting but gives no indication as to the length of her attendance. It is most unlikely that there will be any hint as to what point the meeting had reached by 3.20, when she departed.

4. Much more satisfactory than any of these is:

```
          Mr Wordsworth (Items 4 to 6 only)
```

Cabinet minutes use this final expedient, as shown in these examples from the Cabinet of 10 July 1958, when one of the items being discussed was Defence Organization. The attendance included:

The Rt Hon LORD MILLS, Minister of Power (Item 1)
General Sir GERALD TEMPLER, Chief of the Imperial General Staff
(Item 1)

A subsequent item concerned legal implications of Territorial Waters and the attendance list showed:

The Rt Hon Sir REGINALD MANNINGHAM-BULLER QC, MP,
Attorney General (Item 2)

This leads to the important, if detailed, question of numbering, which is debated in the next chapter.

Description of participants

Whenever a list of names is compiled, friction may be generated, not only by the order in which the names are sequenced, as just discussed, but also by the way in which the people are described. Two principles will guide the minute-taker through this jungle: logic and consistency. Some pitfalls and logical solutions are outlined below.

Initials are safer than first names. The secretary may not know everyone's forenames and it may be unrewardingly time-consuming to ascertain them. Furthermore there is the embarrassment of having someone on the list who is always known by a nickname. It is incongruous and inappropriate to show someone as 'Spud' or 'Chalky' in a formal record of a meeting.

It is a good idea to add the prefix 'Mr' in order to be consistent with the entering of other titles, as they apply. The appellation 'Ms' is now sufficiently well established to be used. Many women feel extremely strongly about it. Some resent it. Others welcome it as a helpful disguise for what they see as the irrelevance, to their work, of their marital status. Military rank is appropriate if the officer is still serving. If he is retired, it will be suitable in certain circumstances; in particular if the officer is generally known by his rank and wishes to be so known, or if he works for a charity or voluntary organization which tends to recruit pensioned service officers on the understanding that they will not require so high a salary.

Such points are demonstrated in this example from a British Red Cross report:

```
PRESENT
The Lady Palmer          (In the Chair)
Mrs B N Cohen SRN        (North)
Mrs M Y Hastings         (South)
Mrs D Percival           (East)
Mrs P M Beck MA          (West including Wales)
Mrs A R Mennie           (Scotland)

In Attendance:
Major-General J Gray     (CMO and Medical Adviser)
Mr J A Duffy             (Director - Activities)
Mrs W Lancaster          (Head of Supply Dept.)
Miss S McCord            (Staff Officer, Youth & Juniors Dept.)
Mrs Richards             (Staff Officer, Activities Dept.)
Miss A Lundegard         (Secretary to Mr Duffy)
Miss B Wood              (Secretary to Mrs Lancaster)
```

It is necessary in minutes of the armed services or relevant government departments to include the notation '(Retired)' after an officer's name, as in:

```
Major-General (Retd) J. Churchill
```

This would seem superfluous in civilian minutes. Decorations and academic awards can normally be omitted: they make an ungainly and cumbersome string at the end of each name.

Summary

The superscription at the top of minutes is of vital importance. It makes clear who was responsible for decisions and the circumstances in which the decisions were taken. For this reason, and because it is the first thing that the reader sees, its contents must be consistent and logical. A set of house-rules giving guidance in this area is highly desirable, even if the structure of the rest of the minutes is left to individual whim or preference.

4 THE TEXT: STANDARD LAYOUT

The minutes themselves consist of a number of items. Each should reflect an item in the agenda, if there is one. Details of the layout of an agenda are set out in Appendix I. No item in the agenda should be omitted from the minutes. If it has been left out of discussion, or if the chairman wishes it to be expunged from the minutes for security reasons, the title must be shown in the minutes with a note to that effect.

Title

Each item should be given a title, such as:

ITEM 3. PERSONNEL
ITEM 4. VEHICLE MAINTENANCE
ITEM 5. SALES STATISTICS
ITEM 6. OVERSEAS CONTRACTS

Components of each item

Each item is likely to comprise of four parts. Sometimes these may justify a paragraph (or more) each, but they will often be run together and covered in a couple of sentences. The constituents are: (a) background; (b) discussion; (c) decision; and (d) action (if any).

Background   A short statement of background will help to set the topic in context. This may be a reminder that a decision is due, or a statement of some problem that has arisen since the last meeting. It could also draw the meeting's attention to a paper which has been submitted etc.

If the background relates to a previous set of minutes, the writer should avoid repeating the detail of those minutes. Probably all that will be necessary is a reference to the previous minute and a one-sentence summary of the topic.

Discussion   This component is the most difficult and requires most judgement. Deciding what to include has been described by one experienced minute-taker in government service as a matter of 'instinct' – hardly a helpful guide to those starting out. The uninitiated should see minutes as a function of the following (sometimes conflicting) factors:

- Length of time spent discussing the item;
- Cost of failure of the item;
- Relationship of the item to others in the agenda;
- Seniority of the contributors.

Length of time   If one item is discussed for four hours and another for ten minutes, the former will inevitably be described at greater length in the minutes. Clearly, with detailed discussion occurring and strong feelings expressed, a proportionate amount of the proceedings should be preserved.

Cost of failure   Sometimes the time factor will contradict the importance of the discussion. An item with enormous public relations significance or financial implications may justify a very detailed record even if everyone agreed the matter quickly. An investment of £500 000 in a critical advertising campaign may have been agreed quickly. However, it will probably justify more space in the minutes than a lengthy aesthetic argument in which managers expressed their preferences for the colour of office stationery.

Relationship of the item to others   Unless the meeting has been badly handled, a glance over the minutes should reflect priorities whereby the most space is given to the most significant items.

Seniority of contributors   However irksome it may seem, there will inevitably be pressure for the contributions of more influential members to be included at greater length than those of the less eminent.

Decision   This is a brief statement of the outcome to the discussion. It should not be amplified by justification.

Action   This will focus responsibility for each decision to a particular individual, including his or her name in the action column. The body of the minutes will state the detailed commitment: the action column will just draw the reader's attention to the person made responsible.

Action columns An action column is complementary to the main text, as in:

Sealed Empty Capsules M H reported that six different types of empty capsules are currently held in stock with one other type possible. M H will ask C H to raise new batch prefixes.	M H

The name of the individual or department responsible does not actually have to appear in the text:

Water Dispensers Cleaning of the dispensers has improved considerably over the past few weeks. M H pointed out that two further dispensers were required.	C R P

The advantage of an action column is that it attracts the readers at once to the items for which they are responsible. The principal disadvantage is that the reader may scan through only for these initials, ignoring other items which ought to be read for information. Furthermore, if there is not much action to be taken, the column can be a waste of space, making the minutes unnecessarily long. An action column 1.5 inches wide will add an extra page to a three-page set of minutes.

Likely important detail

It is impossible to suggest a comprehensive list of topics which should be included in minutes. However, minute-writers should consider carefully whether they can safely omit reference to any of the following which may have been mentioned in discussion: dates; specific sums of money; types of taxation; legal requirements; trade union agreements; names of departments.

Examples

Background This may take the form of a statement of the problem or a brief history of it, as in this example from a waste disposal company: 'It was reported that waste from this customer was blowing out of the container whilst it was in transit.'

A range of openings is demonstrated by the following quotations from the minutes of an administration meeting of a Middle East oil company:

```
Mr Salmeen opened the meeting by welcoming all attendees. The first
subject raised by Mr Salmeen was the safety award for 1983 which was
given . . . He said that JO has been able to achieve this with
co-operation of all JO employees.
```

```
Mr Salmeen reminded Mr Al-Khabbaz about the letter addressed to him
from Mr Zamel regarding the corroded and unsafe cranes in Central
Repair Shop at SSL Camp.
```

On the other hand, in another item the first 11 words seem to be redundant:

```
The next subject discussed was regarding the Periodical Divisional
safety meetings. Mr Salmeen urged the General Services and Material
division to hold their safety meeting periodically.
```

Occasionally background actually appears under a heading, *Background*. More usually it will just be the opening sentence, as in:

```
Dr A has been considering making another presentation to staff during
July.
```

Discussion   This general theme may represent the comments of just one individual rather than a formal debate. For example, the illustration of Dr A's presentation, given above, continues:

```
However, he was of the opinion that holidays and lack of any
important information to pass on would make this exercise a waste of
time as it was his intention to make a presentation during September
when the financial results were announced.
```

Expressions such as

'In discussion $\left\{\begin{array}{l}\text{it was agreed . . .}\\ \text{it was emphasized . . .}\\ \text{it was considered . . .}\\ \text{options were compared . . .}\end{array}\right\}$ '

and so on will often suffice to cover extensive argument, as in the following extracts from Cabinet minutes:

```
In discussion it was recognised that the two most important elements
in the agreement - the size of the lump-sum compensation to be paid
by the Egyptian Government and the formula by which the Egyptian war
damage claims would be waived - could not be inserted in the draft
agreement until progress had been made with the negotiations which
were about to be resumed.
```

```
In discussion the Cabinet were informed that there was unlikely to be
any serious shortage of meat until the following week and that dis-
cussions were proceeding between the employers and the unions on the
possibility of clearing cargoes of butter and cheese as an emergency
operation.
```

```
In discussion there was general agreement with these proposals.
```

The question of attributing comments to individuals is a matter of style and accordingly dealt with in Chapter 6.

Decision   The illustration of the presentation by Dr A, followed above, concludes:

```
There was general agreement that a September presentation would be
acceptable.
```

A British Institute of Management paragraph concludes a five-paragraph item as follows:

```
It was agreed that Divisional Heads should be invited to attend Board
meetings, as had previously been the case, at regular intervals to
give a verbal report on their activities.
```

Action   This part should state the action to be taken, complemented with a note of responsibility in the action column, if there is one, as with these items taken from a section of 'Any Other Business':

```
                                                       ACTION BY

    1.     Heads of Agreement - SEAs to prepare
           draft agreements for their sections.        All
```

```
2.      Unauthorised use of Requisitions - Mr
        Hazleton confirmed investigations in
        hand.                                        JH

3.      Delayed Payment - Gas Oil - Mr Payne
        confirmed action to resolve problem
        areas in hand.                               MP
```

Specific types of item

Minutes of previous meeting
The more formal types of minutes and any of those which constitute part of a series of regular events will invariably start with the minutes of the last meeting. This will generally begin with a simple statement that the minutes were read (or taken as read from the previous minutes). There will then follow a brief note of any amendments which must be made, perhaps as a result of typographical or drafting errors, or because some participants feel that they have been wrongly or inadequately represented. An example of such a correction from a transport company's minutes follows:

```
1/12/85   MINUTES OF PREVIOUS MEETING
          Minutes of previous meeting held on 21 November 1985.
          Minute No 16/9/85, item 4, should read: 1986/87 not
          85/86.
```

There is no need to be pedantic about amendments, and usually no need to give reasons. A clear reference to the sub-paragraph or item to be amended and the particular change of words required is all that is necessary. Sometimes, if a longer explanation is needed, the revised passage may have to be attached as a separate sheet. The Council of The Chartered Association of Certified Accountants shows this in its minutes:

```
COMMITTEE'S TERMS OF REFERENCE

For the Committee's information, and further to minute 2 of the last
meeting, Council at its meeting of 7 November, 1985 accepted General
Purposes Committee's recommendation that two amendments be made to
International Affairs Committee's terms of reference in order to
reflect more accurately its activities. A copy of the revised terms
of reference is attached at page 9.
```

Absence of any discussion All the items in the agenda must be reflected in the minutes. If there has been no discussion of a subject, this must be stated under the appropriate heading. The transport company's minutes quoted above continue as follows:

```
2/12/85    REVIEW OF MEETINGS
           Nothing to report
```

Courtesies to members It will often be appropriate to mention specific achievements or other important incidents in the lives of members at the meeting. This may be the award of a decoration, marriage or - more directly relevant - retirement from the committee. In all cases such simple acknowledgements must be recorded, as in this British Red Cross example:

```
Retiring Member

The Vice Chairman expressed the Society's gratitude to Mrs R.A.E.
Herbert, who was attending her last Finance Committee meeting on
retiring from the Council, and consequently from the Chairman's and
Finance Committees.
```

Statement of positions in detail Sometimes an item may state a fairly complex but routine position, such as staff levels, sales performance, organization charts and so on. It is entirely acceptable to make only a brief reference in the minutes and then to attach the display material as an appendix. This can be a simple '(See Appendix A)' or it can be rather lengthier, as in this case from the Student Services Committee of the Chartered Association of Certified Accountants:

```
An analysis of the current graduates of the Association, by year of
completion of the examinations, is attached on page 4.
```

The handling of appendices is treated in full in Chapter 9.

Any other business There is nothing wrong with having a section on Any Other Business. There is no justification or logic in the view that inclusion of such a section is in some way undisciplined. In most subject matters, problems - even crises - may arise between the distribution of the agenda and the meeting. If necessary, at a formal meeting such as an AGM, the Chairman can require advance notice of such additional business and refuse to include anything without this notification.

It is convenient if Any Other Business:

● Has a heading or lead-in phrase;

● Consists of a number of discrete items.

**Date of
next
meeting**

Although the Agenda will provide details of the next meeting in due course, as described in Appendix I, it is important that a full explanation of the date and place of the next meeting should be given at the end of the minutes. This is the only intimation that anyone not at the current meeting will have of these details until the agenda is distributed a few days before the next meeting.

Furthermore, if there is a great deal of tedious discussion about individual preferences for the next meeting - something which most often is entirely unnecessary - the date eventually decided on may have been obscured by argument. The Red Cross minutes quoted earlier ended with:

```
838         Date and Place of Next Meeting
            Tuesday, 29th May 1984 at 9 Grosvenor Crescent,
            London SW1, at 5.00 pm.
```

Sometimes it is appropriate to state that no date has been fixed, as in another set of Red Cross minutes:

```
No date was fixed for another meeting of the Working Party.
```

Complete examples

The following are a number of annotated complete minute items which demonstrate the principles described in this chapter.

Example 1 (British Red Cross)

BACKGROUND	–	Mrs Hastings raised the question of circulars on uniform not reaching her through the Branch.
DISCUSSION	–	Mr Duffy expressed concern over this situation.
DECISION	–	It was felt, however, that this was a matter for the Branch Affairs Committee to discuss under the general heading of communication.
ACTION	–	Mr Duffy undertook to send copies of any circular issued by his Dept on the subject of uniform to the members of the Working Party.

Example 2 (Glaxo Operations)

BACKGROUND	–	It was stated that a Numerical Code Input Device is available for attachment to line
DISCUSSION/ EXPLANATION	–	machinery; this translates numerical input Laetus codes to their binary equivalents and feeds these directly to the bar code reader.
DECISION	–	It was agreed that this equipment would be beneficial.
ACTION	–	The purchase of the device for appropriate lines is to be recommended to all Department Heads.

Example 3 (Tyne and Wear Passenger Transport Executive)
This demonstrates the position at greater length.

M402 *LOW FELL COACHES*

BACKGROUND – Mr. Hutchinson referred to the recent decision by the Traffic Commissioners to grant for one year the application of Low Fell Coaches for a licence to operate a service between Allerdene and St. Thomas Street. The P.T.E. and N.G.T. had also been requested not to implement the service as reductions seemed necessary to compensate for estimated loss of revenue, and the respective Traffic Managers were now in course of preparing advice to the Chairman of the Transport Committee on whether to appeal, such a course of action being favoured by the Operations Liaison Group.

DISCUSSION – Mr. Brindle expressed the view that an appeal would be worthwhile, stating, however, that in order to maintain credibility, the proposed cuts in services for the Gateshead area should be proceeded with. Mr. Ballinger thought it was essential to appeal against the decision, whatever the likely outcome, so to preserve staff morale. On the question of service reductions, he felt it was not advisable to introduce these prior to the appeal hearing. Mr. Hutchinson stated, in support of this view, that the effects of the grant would be better known in about three or four months' time and that, as far as the Appeal was concerned, it would be reasonable to reserve the position for the time being as regards to the

		implementation of the service cuts. An application to introduce these could, however, be proceeded with in the meantime.
DECISION	–	It was agreed, therefore, that the question of an appeal would be left for the legal advisers and P.T.E./N.G.T. Traffic Managers to deal with, it being anticipated that they would shortly be in a position to fully brief the Chairman of Public Transport Committee
ACTION	–	on the matter. The operations Liaison Group would, in parallel, consider whether there were any further measures of a commercial and competitive nature which could be implemented, in order to offset the likely revenue losses brought about by the granting of the application by Low Fell Coaches.

This example of the format is lengthy both because a more attributive style is appropriate and because the more elaborate background and complex course of action had to be described.

Example 4 (Joint Operations Wafra)

BACKGROUND	–	Mr Salmeen expressed his deep concern about the fast speeding of vehicles on the roads. He stressed that all JO employees should drive vehicles at a safe speed and adopt the habit of using safety belts. He
DISCUSSION	–	further advised F&S personnel to start following these requirements as an example to others. Also he advised all concerned to go through the booklet provided by transport explaining safe driving procedure. Mr Salmeen
DECISION/ ACTION	–	advised that no car should be moved from the accident spot till investigation is completed by local authorities. He also advised that JO F&S provides a suggestion form for use of the employees, with boxes available at all divisions for any safety comments.

In this example the abbreviations JO (meaning Joint Operations) and F&S (meaning Fire Safety) had been introduced earlier. The minutes were written by a secretary whose first language was not English working for an oil-producing organization that uses English as its *lingua franca*. The example demonstrates how the sequence remains valid even when there is only one significant contributor to an item.

Example 5 (British Institute of Management)
Sometimes the decision and action will be described at much greater length, as in this illustration:

BACKGROUND	–	*FUTURE OF THE INFORMATION SERVICES* The Chairman invited Dr Ron French to introduce his proposals for the future of the Information Services contained in paper BIMF (82)34. Dr French explained that the plan for modernising the information services, which had been presented to the Board at its previous meeting, now had been costed. He
DISCUSSION	–	reminded the Board that the main purpose of the proposals was to provide a better and more up-to-date service for BIM members rather than to provide cost saving. He added that under the proposals modernisation would begin in 1983 but that implementation of the proposals depended upon phase II or relocation and that the timing of the charge would be affected by the timing of phase II of relocation.
DECISION	–	Mr Nicholson said that Finance Committee had considered Dr French's proposals and had agreed that modernisation should take place as proposed. The Board endorsed this view, approving the proposals set out in the paper. It was noted that the Board would be kept informed of progress.
ACTION	–	Thanks were expressed to Dr French for his assistance and advice; it was noted that Dr French would be continuing to act for BIM in negotiations concerning the new equipment.

Here the action is not so much a series of points agreed by the meeting, rather more a record of the *status quo*.

Summary

A minute item should be seen as consisting of four components. The Background will set the topic in context and possibly link it with earlier meetings. The Discussion will be summarized. The Decision will be stated in as clear and uncompromising language as reflects the tone of the meeting. Any specific Action will be described, along with the names of organizations, departments or individuals responsible for taking it.

The amount of the discussion included in the minutes will depend on the importance, length of discussion and status of the contributors.

An action column may be helpful, provided that it does not lead to unreasonably selective reading.

All items in the agenda must appear in a set of minutes even if no discussion took place.

Congratulations and other courtesies to those present should appear at the beginning or end of the minutes. The minutes will normally close with particulars of the next meeting.

5 THE TEXT: NON-STANDARD LAYOUTS

Different traditions in different working environments may suggest alternate layouts of the minute items.

Placing of action

In particular differing formats for recording the action are sometimes felt to be appropriate, the following being the more common variations.

Writing the action below

> The problem with intermittent noise cannot be duplicated on the Galway switch fitted with the returned SBC packs. Further investigation is required into the configuration of the SBC system and confirmation required as to whether the noise is still being experienced in Germany.
>
> <u>Action.</u> Confirm noise still being experienced by SBC.

(Northern Telecom)

Action absorbed into the text

> ...nothing should be done until they have the opportunity of firming up a policy in relation to the Government's intended measures.

(Tyne and Wear PTE)

Action column to the left

Some house styles call for placing the action column to the left:

```
ACTION
```

as in the minutes of Systems Division, Willis Faber & Dumas.

Timed action columns

Where meetings are held frequently and the action required is time-sensitive, a further column giving the date by which action is required may be desirable. This is used by Bayer (UK), the pharmaceutical company:

```
                           ACTION      DUE DATE

1.  Registration Status    HL          2/3

2.  Launch Conference      LS          9/3
```

Formal record of something noted

There will be occasions in highly official minutes, particularly in governmental or quasi-governmental bodies, when it will be necessary to record that a comment (such as congratulations) has been formally noted. For example, in minutes of the Board of Directors of the Council for Small Industries in Rural Areas:

```
(b)  County Committee - Minute 15 (a) (iii)
```
```
The Board congratulated the Chairman on the quality of the County
Committee Chairmen he was recruiting.
                                               This was NOTED.
```

The minute in the title refers to an earlier set of minutes which was being discussed at the Board meeting.

Likewise, in this illustration from the British Red Cross Society:

```
828  The Minutes of the Sixty-Ninth Meeting of the Finance Committee
     (circulated) were confirmed and signed.

829  Cash Flow Statements for the months of February and March 1984
     (circulated) were received and noted.

830  Statements of Legacies, Quota Receipts and Donations for the
     months of February and March 1984
     (circulated) were received and noted.
```

In such cases, where there are other documents not actually attached to the minutes, a note at the end will be helpful, as follows (also Red Cross):

```
NOTE:
Copies of all papers circulated and tabled are in the Minute Book.
```

Inclusion of a vote result

Sometimes - particularly in formal meetings or where a very contentious or sensitive issue is being considered - it may be important to record the vote. This can be especially significant in board meetings, meetings of shareholders and any other contexts in which major changes of policy are debated. Examples might be:

- Carried by acclamation;
- Carried 28–14 with 2 abstentions;
- Vote 59–31 in favour (excluding abstentions) but rejected as lacking the necessary two-thirds majority;
- Vote 10–10, chairman used casting vote in favour.

It may also be desirable to include the names of scrutineers where they have been used in a secret ballot. In a more public context, the names of tellers (for the 'Ayes' and the 'Noes') are recorded in Hansard after a Parliamentary vote.

Traditional abbreviations based on Latin phrases, such as *nem con (nemine contradicente)*, no one opposing, and *nem dis (nemine dissentiente)*, nobody dissenting, are wretchedly dated and have no place in modern minutes.

Amount of detail

Sometimes a much more crisp, succinct set of minutes items will be favoured. The format of Background – Discussion – Decision – Action advised in the previous chapter will be too laboured. The following items deal with public transport facilities:

```
WORKING TIMES
The work is to be completed during restricted night working hours,
ie 0100 to 0400 hours daily.
```

Of slightly greater length but equally concisely expressed is:

```
PROTECTION

Protection to prevent public access to storage and working area to be
included. All areas lifted during restricted hours shall be relayed.
No exposed areas shall be permitted between visits to site.
```

Division of items

The way in which the items are divided will also vary from one company to another. The division of a set of minutes into discrete items is conventional, segregating the various topics and drawing attention to the various areas of discussion. To this end, each agenda item normally demands a separate full paragraph in the minutes. Minutes in the administration of Systems Division of Willis Faber & Dumas simplify this by having a section for matters arising and a section for new business, both suitably subdivided:

```
1.  APOLOGIES

2.  MINUTES OF PREVIOUS MEETING

3.  MATTERS ARISING

    3.1 Sign on Computer Room Door

    3.2 Restaurant Facilities

    3.3 Car Park Exit Flaps

    3.4 Swimming Pool - Signing-in of Guests

4.  NEW BUSINESS

    4.1 Car Park Ramps

    4.2 25 Years Service Gift

    4.3 Flooding of Paths to Greyfriars
```

New business is more usually presented as a number of separate items (4, 5 and 6). The number of levels in the numbering system should always be kept as simple as possible. However, as there are only three in the example above, the format shown works quite satisfactorily. It is worth noting in this example that the sub-entries in Sections 3 and 4 are suitably specific. For example, item 3.4 is not just called 'Swimming Pool': it has a helpful sub-title, 'Signing-in of Guests'. Item 4.3 is not just 'Paths to Greyfriars' (one of the company's buildings) but more accurately 'Flooding of Paths to Greyfriars'.

Format for highly formal minutes

Highly formal minutes will just show the decision reached and those who reached it. The formality of any discussion means that it is a waste of time recording it in the minutes. An example is the proceedings of a Parliamentary Committee (Figure 5.1).

PROCEEDINGS OF THE COMMITTEE RELATING TO THE REPORT

MONDAY, 27 FEBRUARY, 1984

Members present:

Mr Robert Sheldon, in the Chair

Mr Dale Campbell-Savours	Mr William O'Brien
Mr Eric Cockeram	Mr George Park
Mr Eric Deakins	Sir Michael Shaw
Mr Michael Latham	Mr Michael Shersby
Mr Michael Morris	Mr Fred Silvester

Sir Gordon Downey, KCB, was further examined.

The Committee deliberated.

Mr C H A Judd was called in and further examined.

The Report of the Wardale enquiry into recent cases of fraud and corruption in the Property Services Agency was considered.

Sir Geoffrey Wardale, KCB; Mr A G Herron, Touche Ross and Co; Mr A Montague Alfred, Chief Executive, Mr Geoffrey Chipperfield, Deputy Chief Executive, and Mr Alan Atherton, Under Secretary, Property Services Agency; were called in and examined.

[Adjourned till Wednesday at a quarter past Four o'clock.

Figure 5.1 Proceedings of the Committee (formal parliamentary committee minutes)

Summary

Different meetings will call for different formats.

Action columns may be replaced by other types of recording: perhaps writing the names of responsible individuals below, perhaps adding such details as the date by which it should be completed. Some situations will call for the recording of a vote result.

Complex items will benefit from extensive subdivision.

6 STYLE

Style is a particular way of doing things. It may be based on nationality or culture or be associated with a specific profession or trade. It may be a format or approach laid down by a particular company or organization or simply be a personal preference.

There are analogies with dress. Certain styles of dress are suitable for certain occasions and certain personalities. They are subject to fashion. Some extremes are unacceptable on almost all occasions; others are acceptable in almost every context.

In the same way there will be variations in styles of minutes: some, covering informal and ephemeral topics, may deserve a fairly light-weight, informal style; others, with weightier consequences and longer lives, may demand more formality. Most importantly, minutes must be recorded in a consistent style and be unambiguous.

Minutes should be an objective record of a meeting. By writing as impersonally as possible, the minute-writer can produce an impartial and credible record. Sudden and dramatic changes in style are not appropriate. They will startle and surprise the reader. This can be admirable in a novel or a tabloid newspaper, but a set of minutes is more clinical.

Paragraph size

Short paragraphs are appropriate for minutes, making them easier to absorb or read selectively. They also make it easier to refer back to particular parts of the document later. Apart from a change of style during the Second World War, when an exceptionally wide range of topics was dealt with in very short, succinct paragraphs, Cabinet minutes have been characterized for the whole of this century by vast paragraphs frequently running to 60 lines of typescript. Joan Bailey, one of the civil servants responsible for taking the minutes, writes of this style: 'It is still usual to record a contribution in a single paragraph though in some cases a series of paragraphs is used, where this would assist the reader.'

Sentence length

A Victorian length of sentence is no longer appropriate. A century ago, elaborate, convoluted structures in the manner of Latin sentences were influential in business writing. Quite the opposite style is appropriate to minutes, where each sentence should contain one single idea. The meaning should be immediately obvious and not require a second reading.

As a crude rule of thumb, three subordinate phrases or clauses should be regarded as a maximum for each sentence. Rules of thumb are always suspect in respect of writing style, inhibiting fluency. They are particularly dangerous with regard to sentence length. However the wisdom of the guideline is borne out by a few examples. Using a normal reading speed, the reader may stumble over the following sentence and have to tackle it a second time, at least.

> The Company took a serious view on the matter with regard to safety of others and to the nature of the plant, ie chemical plants containing highly flammable liquids, etc, and the pharmaceuticals areas using high speed equipment, etc. The Chairman made it clear that drunkenness could not be tolerated.

The important point in the sentence is that drunkenness cannot be tolerated. This should be dignified by a separate sentence, as could the characteristics of the plant. The extract could then read:

> Highly flammable liquids and the use of high speed equipment gave the plant a number of safety hazards. It was important to attach a high priority to safety in the company. Drunkenness could not be tolerated.

The following sentence is clearly too tortuous:

> At the year end this year, it was not until the beginning of November that all accounts had been returned, next year the committee would like to see more effort from Section Treasurers so that the year end accounts can be produced with less trouble.

This is grammatically two sentences, which should be separated by a full-stop between 'had been returned' and 'next year'. The opening phrase, 'At the year end this year' is also ungainly and could easily be telescoped to 'at this year end'.

A simpler sentence structure is called for in minutes than in other writing. In many contexts the following sentence would be acceptable:

```
Some discussion took place on this issue, Mr Walker pointing out that
the matter was already being considered by the Finance Liaison Group,
and that a number of divergent views had been expressed as to the
method for recharging in respect of certain items.
```

In minutes, however, this would preferably be divided into three sentences:

```
Some discussion took place on this issue. Mr Walker pointed out that
the matter was already being considered by the Finance Liaison Group.
A number of divergent views had been expressed as to the method for
recharging in respect of certain items.
```

Sub-paragraphing can be an excellent way of itemizing points which would otherwise form a rather cumbersome list in the same sentence. The paragraph quoted above goes on:

```
Aspects which were currently being looked at included:

(a)  equipment owned by one organisation and maintained by another;

(b)  equipment owned by the P.T.E. and on loan to the Companies;

(c)  supplies and services provided in the normal course of
     operations;

(d)  supplies and services provided solely as a result of integration;

(e)  questions of premises and other wider issues.
```

Ambiguity

In exceptional circumstances, minutes can be written in note form without finite verbs. However sentences are generally the simplest item of complete thought and anything less may produce ambiguity and confusion. Consider, for example:

> H2 temperature too high. Shaw responsible. Last satisfactory 1 December 1989. Next servicing 1 June. Shaw notifying.

Doubtless the drift of this would be clear to those who had attended the meeting but for anyone else a number of questions suggest themselves: For what precisely was Shaw responsible? Exactly when should he do the notifying? What information is he to notify? Is the servicing due on 1 June or is it going to take place then?

Such ambiguity is likely to be avoided if the minutes are recorded in full conventional sentences, each with a subject and a finite verb. At least, then, the risk of misunderstanding will be minimized. Dearborn Chemicals get away with an incomplete sentence in an important note:

```
1. X -- reported to be stopping bottle service from 1st January
   1981. Confirmation required.
```

The following guidelines will help to remove ambiguity:

● Avoid excessively long sentences.
● Avoid vague or confusing use of pronouns (especially 'it').
● Avoid too many relative (or other subordinate) clauses.
● Avoid repetition of the same conjunction 'who . . . who . . .' (or 'but . . . but . . . but . . .' or 'if . . . if . . .').

The sentence below might read more easily without the two relative clauses 'which . . . which . . .' In fact, greater clarity could easily be achieved by dividing the sentence at the conjunction 'and'.

```
London Brick Products would supply a portable substation which at
present is surplus to their requirements, and would also continue to
supply HV electricity via an existing cable which will require diver-
ting at its substation end.
```

These problems – particularly misleading use of pronouns - usually stem from adding material to draft minutes and not reading them through afterwards. When anything is added, not only the whole sentence but the whole paragraph should be read again. This will ensure firstly that it makes the sense that the writer intends; secondly that there is no unwitting repetition of words; and thirdly that there is no danger of the pronouns inadvertently referring to something that is not intended. Sometimes, in a small-scale internal meeting, note-form sentences will suffice as the meaning may be clear to every conceivable reader.

Unnecessary ambiguity is also often introduced by physical descriptions, such as: 'Turning to the bar he thanked the bar stewards of the year.' The phrase, 'turning to the bar' is irrelevant. It is the sort of thing which the speaker might have said when making his comments, in order to change the direction of the listeners' attention. Minutes are not designed to include such descriptive transitions: a new paragraph with the words 'bar stewards' in the first line would suffice. Alternatively a sub-heading 'Bar' could be introduced. 'Turning to the bar...' is an example of unnecessary padding. These are natural, and sometimes important, adjuncts in oral expression, but phrases such as 'Finally, but not least...' and 'Having said all this...' usually have no place in a set of minutes.

Sub-headings within an agenda item (as in the case of the suggested sub-title 'Bar' above) often help to produce an economical style of expression, as can be found in Dearborn Chemicals:

> Bonus Bonds: Claims continue to be received under the present incen-
> tive schemes.

Attributability

Many minute-takers feel that it is important to attribute comments to individual speakers. This is a laborious style which makes for heavy reading and may sometimes even obscure important points. It is an approach particularly favoured in environments (often educational or artistic) in which individual responsibility is important. However, even here it is generally unnecessary. Exceptions are:

- If particularly strong reservations are expressed by one individual about something which is agreed by everyone else.
- If the speaker asks for his or her name to be recorded in a particular context.
- Where participants are representing constituents of any kind, for example county or district councillors or trade union representatives.

For example:

> In reply to Mrs H—, Mr E— would investigate the need for 2 S— buses and any other ways of economizing the use of the buses.

or the more important personal involvement in the following:

> Miss — wished to know at which forum she should raise the issue of complaints about the canteen. Mr — asked that any complaints of this nature be routed through him as he has line responsibility.

The question of attribution can cause more problems to meeting secretaries than any other aspect of style. It is also often the matter on which participants impose most pressure. It is relevant therefore to examine in detail two paragraphs from minutes of the British Red Cross in which a useful compromise has been achieved. The example has been chosen as the independent nature of the Red Cross makes impartial but accurate reporting essential.

> A general discussion took place on matters of procedure, as a result of which a number of points were agreed upon for issue to Branches by the Director of Activities in the form of a guidance circular to be issued to Branches, a copy of which is appended to these minutes.

```
Several further points were raised and discussed by members. Mr Duffy
raised the question of the men's caps - and asked about the possi-
bility of adding some gold braid - which could give authority to Red
Cross personnel when out on duty. The extra expense was considered to
be a major factor. General Gray suggested the idea of clip-on tabs.
Mr Duffy showed an example of an identification badge to the members
```

In the first illustration all that matters is that discussion has led to general agreement. Only the Director of Activities is mentioned individually as he has to take action. In the second example, two participants are mentioned by name. Mr Duffy raised the issue of caps. Clearly he felt this to be important and his introduction of the subject is acknowledged in the minute. General Gray put forward a new idea which could significantly alter the character of the Red Cross uniform. So although the relevant working party now has to consider the matter, Gray is credited with proposing this novel idea. In both cases only such attributions as are necessary and helpful are included.

Where the names or job-titles of contributors are included in the text of minutes, they can be left in normal type, as in the Red Cross example above. However when the minute items are long and include many names, they may be highlighted in some way. Cabinet minutes used to do this by underlining, as in this example from a meeting of 10 July 1958 when defence organization was discussed by heads of the armed services.

```
The First Sea Lord spoke in favour of the organization proposed in
the draft White Paper and supported the views expressed by the Chair-
man of the Chiefs of Staff Committee.
```

Such titles are now shown in BLOCK CAPITALS in Cabinet minutes.

Generally, writing minutes in the form of questions is to be avoided, as it tends towards too informal a style. But sometimes in internal minutes, where answers to definite questions are required, it can be an economical arrangement. The following passage from minutes of the Centre for British Teachers (providing British and Australian teachers to the government of Malaysia) demonstrates this. The style (as indicated by the use of the word 'kids' and the note form) is informal, which is acceptable in this case. The questions certainly focus the mind.

```
EFFECTS OF RAMADAN ON SCHOOL LIFE
J K requested Area Secretaries to ask their groups to summarise their
experiences on the effects of fasting on their school life, eg
```

```
    i. Are the kids more noticeably tired?
   ii. School canteen still functions as normal?
  iii. Smoking, drinking and eating habits?
```

A good example of a workmanlike style of minutes is to be seen in these paragraphs from a public transport company:

```
b) Supervisory Training - Management Skills

It is recognised that training in general management skills for Sup-
ervisors is essential. It has become apparent that Supervisors need
to be made aware of their role. Miss Olive said that she had had dis-
cussions with John Hearn regarding the needs and implementation of
management training for Supervisors. Proposals have been submitted by
one group of consultants but these had not been found to meet the
company's requirements. And arrangements were in hand to discuss the
matter with two further companies.

Mr Allcock said that the Permanent Way was devising a vocational
training course for Supervisors as it had become clear that some form
of training is needed for existing Supervisors.
```

Given that 'Permanent Way' is a departmental title, this makes excellent, lucid reading. The sentences are of reasonable length without being simplistic. The wording is apt and meaningful, although the inconsistency of 'John Hearn' – as opposed to 'Miss Olive' and 'Mr Allcock' – is a minor irritation.

There are various ways of describing participants in minutes, the most common being:

- *Mr Wilde, Mrs Austen.* This seems slightly formal by modern conventions, but will never actually give offence.
- *John Galsworthy, Emily Brontë.* This is equally clear (or clearer as people of the same surname will not be confused). However in some environments, senior people or visitors from outside may not be comfortable with the intimacy of first names. (The confusing and regrettable vogue for using forenames on their own should be avoided.)
- *WS, VW.* Initials are helpfully concise. They irritate some people and, with large meetings, readers will need to consult the list of attenders to interpret them. Confusion may occur in cases where people have the same initials.

Whatever system is chosen, it must be used consistently for all participants unless there is a good reason for some clear and undisputed division of appellations (such as initials for internal members and some more elaborate form for visitors).

Itemizing sub-paragraphs is a valuable way of presenting substantial amounts of important detail. The topic of dress in the Red Cross generates much detailed discussion and some strong feelings. The minutiae which surface in these exchanges can usefully be recorded in this way:

```
Miss McCord reported on reactions among Youth and Juniors, primary
among these being the question of expense. The following points
emerged.

1.  There was a query on the sizing of tabards for Youth and Junior
    members, as the smallest size currently provided does not always
    fit the smaller girls. Mrs Lancaster suggested that a size 28"
    tabard could be made up to be tested and worn as a trial
    experiment on sizing.

2.  There had also been a query on whether qualification flashes
    should be worn on navy blue melton jackets, as some girls still
    have them, and also on the boys' navy blue melton overshirt. It
    was agreed that qualification flashes could be worn on the old
    style melton jackets/overshirts.

3.  The question of flashes on lupin blue dresses was raised. The
    members agreed that this was not possible, because of the size.
```

Cross-references to other documents can be achieved most economically simply by citing the paragraph numbers of the original. This can be important if the meeting has been discussing a report, as for example in this paragraph from minutes of the Council for Small Industries in Rural Areas:

```
The Working Party's report and the recommendations were APPROVED sub-
ject to the following paragraphs being amended:-
4.3.3 (as agreed at the meeting), 4.9.6 (delete), 4.12.4, 4.12.5,
4.12.6, 4.12.10, 4.13.1, 4.13.2 (delete), 4.13.3, 4.13.4, 4.13.5,
4.13.6, 5.12.1, 5.12.10 and 5.12.11.
```

The simple comment '(as agreed at the meeting)' against sub-sub-paragraph 4.3.3 is probably sufficient if the amendment was obvious or non-controversial.

Tense

A wide variety of tenses may be used. When future events have been formally agreed, the form 'would...' is frequently appropriate as in:

Ownership

The ownership of the new electrical supply would be as follows:-

London Brick Products would own the HV cable and substation up to
and including the MV insolator switch, thereafter all MV cabling
and electrical equipment would be owned by LBC.

The imperfect tense ('was', 'were') is frequently used, as in this extract
from the British Institute of Management which also illustrates a proper
use of the passive (so often unjustly disparaged):

Interest was expressed in the current numbers of Individual Members
overseas. It was agreed that an analysis of overseas members by
country of origin would be circulated with the Minutes.

On the other hand the past tense ('said...', 'outlined...', 'explained...')
is useful to link speakers and their comments, as in this short passage
from Cabinet minutes:

. . . the Prime Minister said that it was evident that the Administration was unlikely to take any vigorous steps in the United States.

Numbering

There are two aspects of numbering or itemizing which are relevant
to minutes: minute or item numbers, and sub-paragraph numbering.
These are important as they provide a means both for cross-referencing
within the minutes and for referring to items in subsequent sets of
minutes and other documents.

Perpetual numbering In this system, the first set of minutes starts with 1, 2, 3 and the
series continues *ad infinitum*. This has the disadvantage of the numbering
eventually becoming unwieldy, with as many as five figures.

New series for each set of minutes This means that the sequence 1, 2, 3, is started again for each set of
minutes. The result is a more concise expression to number each
minute, but a cumbersome format for cross-reference: 'Minute 14 dated
10 May 1988' (as opposed to the unique 'Minute 267').

New series starting every year This involves starting a new sequence at the beginning of each January
and incorporating the last two digits of the year in the minute number.
Thus the series might run 91/64, 91/65, 91/66, 91/67 with the 67th

and last minute of 1991 at the end of December. The sequence will then start 92/1, 92/2 etc at the beginning of the next year. To many people this seems less cumbersome and more specific. A subsequent reference to such a minute makes it clear at once from what year the minute is taken. It is therefore particularly suitable for those series of minutes which run for several years.

In some of its monthly minutes a public transport organization uses a combined system:

1/12/90 MINUTES OF PREVIOUS MEETING
2/12/90 REVIEW OF MEETINGS
3/12/90 STAFF MATTERS
4/12/90 ANY OTHER BUSINESS

In this 90 represents the year 1990. The 12 indicates that it is the December meeting. The numbers 1, 2, 3, 4, are the items of the December meeting. The advantage of this system is that each item indicates precisely which monthly meeting is involved. Its disadvantage is the cumbersome size of each number.

For sub-paragraphing, the two most usual systems are *lettering of sub-paragraphs:*

1   . . . .
2   . . . .
3   . . . .
        a   . . . .
        b   . . . .
        c   . . . .
4   . . . .
        a   . . . .
        b   . . . .
5   . . . .
6   . . . .

and a *decimal system:*

1   . . . .
2   . . . .
3   . . . .
        3.1   . . . .
        3.2   . . . .
        3.3   . . . .
4   . . . .
        4.1   . . . .
        4.2   . . . .
5   . . . .
6   . . . .

Division beyond sub-paragraphs is unlikely to be necessary or desirable in most minutes. Sub-paragraphs can be signalled by dashes or bullet points. This is simple and precludes renumbering should the order of points be changed during drafting. For example:

The company would open new branches at
- Milton Keynes
- Cwmbran
- Livingstone
- Basingstoke
- Swindon

Punctuation

Underlining is rather a ham-fisted form of emphasis; usually greater accuracy can be achieved by more specific word choice. However, sometimes a short, seemingly insignificant word may carry disproportionate importance in a sentence and will need the help of underlining. The following paragraph from Dearborn Chemicals deals with aspects of commercial integrity and etiquette. Here the underlining is justified.

```
In the interests of Dearborn's integrity as a company, the names of
customers or prospects must be obliterated from competition quotes,
C.S.R.s, letters, etc, before circulation within Dearborn.
```

Inverted commas should be used sparingly and not to clarify the meaning of words. Only direct quotations and document titles are likely to justify them. Here they are used by Dearborn to show a colloquial use but even so are probably unnecessary:

```
Continuous blowdown/heat recovery: provision of suitable 'glossy'
literature is being investigated.
```

Notes

Sometimes notes are added after the meeting. This can be done by use of an asterisk, as by London Brick Landfill who placed this note at the foot of the page:

```
2. London Brick Landfill will fund* the following items . . ..
   * Subject to SE approval
```

Dearborn Chemicals put an important correction in brackets at the end of the item so that it could not be overlooked:

```
Y —— reported to be in Receivership. Confirmation required. (Infor-
mation since reported as false.)
```

The claim of receivership by the competitor company had to go into the minutes and doubtless generated much excitement at the meeting. However, it was extremely important that the false rumour should be scotched in a way that nobody would miss.

Summary

The style of any written material will depend on the context, the subject-matter, the type of meeting, the formality of the occasion, and the seniority and attitude of the participants.

The style must be consistent and unambiguous.

Attributing comments to individuals will be exceptional.

A style of numbering should be chosen which is appropriate to the structure of the minutes, the length of the items and the diversity of the subject-matter.

7 VOCABULARY

The great diversity of vocabulary in the English language is seldom more important or more relevant than in minutes. In just a dozen lines or so the author of the minutes must do justice to all the disagreement, repetition and acrimony of perhaps an hour's debate.

The importance of tiny differences in meaning is demonstrated by the following:

He	said	(bland)
	stated	(more formal)
	argued	(faced with difficulty)
	contested	(confrontational)
	emphasized	(allowing no opposition)
	reinforced	(a second time)
	stressed	(involving effort)
	urged	(trying to get others to agree)
	declared	(theatrical)
	mentioned	(incidental)

By choosing a particular word to describe the introduction of an idea to a meeting, one can convey the tone of the exchange. The effect of adverbs is also important. Consider the impact of 'strongly', 'emphatically', 'forcefully'. These can be valuable tools in making the description of a participant's contribution more vivid.

The following quotations are also instructive: 'X expressed his view strongly.' The adverb at the end is enough to convey the tone and atmosphere of the meeting. 'In a heated discussion the meeting examined all aspects of the problem.' The word 'heated' conveys the expression of strong feelings, and 'all aspects of the problem' implies a wide-ranging and exhaustive discussion.

In the following example one word again carries the spirit of the occasion: 'Mr Y said that his department could not tolerate the situation any longer.' The word 'tolerate' suggests that his department is near breaking-point over the issue. This is probably an exaggeration but it reflects his strength of feeling.

49

There are two types of reference books which will help in the best choice of words. Thesauri will prompt the writer looking for a more precise synonym. Dictionaries will provide current definitions.

Thesauri

The best known thesaurus is Roget's. It retains both its originator's name and its French pronunciation in tribute to Peter Mark Roget who produced the first edition in 1852.

The book is arranged in two parts. A form of index takes up the last third of the book; it shows the principal words and lists various aspects under each term. For example, *say* leads to *affirm*, *speak* or *decree*. Each of these sub-divisions is shown as leading to a particular paragraph in the main section (first two-thirds) of the book. In that part are to be found extensive collections of quasi-synonyms.

The range of words is enormous. For example, the paragraph showing *affirm* gives 168 words and phrases. Clearly the spread of meaning over so many items is vast, and many of the terms offered in a thesaurus paragraph are only loosely related to the original meaning. A thesaurus should therefore be used as an *aide-mémoire*. No word from a thesaurus should ever be chosen unless the minute-writer has seen it alive and well, doing its proper job in a natural environment.

Dictionaries

An up-to-date dictionary should be used to check:

● *Whether a word is in current usage*. As the language develops, new words come into use and have to earn their place in a dictionary. Only then should they be used in minutes.
● *Whether a word has any restrictive label*. Sometimes words newly shown in a dictionary are labelled 'slang' or 'colloquial' suggesting they are not suitable for formal use. Such words should be avoided in minutes. Some dictionaries, such as *Longman's Dictionary of the English Language*, have helpful notes on usage for the more controversial entries. While these are disparaged by more conventional lexicographers, they can be extremely useful and are invaluable to those minute-writers who do not have English as their first language.
● *What a word's current meaning is*. Words change their meaning, sometimes imperceptibly, the whole time. A current dictionary will indicate how the serious reader should interpret a word. For example: Can *unique* be used in its extended sense, meaning 'fairly unusual'? Can *incredible* be used to mean 'hard to believe, surprising'? Does *literally* have an acceptable new meaning, 'with a bit of exaggeration'?

The minutes should no more be written in Victorian English than in the Middle English of Chaucer. It is important to choose up-to-date wording which can be understood by all readers, without being over-trendy. The most suitable guidance will be found in the following: *Concise Oxford Dictionary*, *Chambers English Dictionary*, *Collins English Dictionary* and *Longman's Dictionary of the English Language*.

Formal minutes with a wide circulation, possibly even publication, will demand a formal vocabulary. Informal minutes such as those of a sports and social club or a village darts league will permit more informal vocabulary. Thus the canteen committee can say, '. . . so that the year-end accounts can be produced with less hassle'. 'Hassle' is shown in the *Concise Oxford Dictionary* as colloquial and even in the more progressive *Longman's Dictionary of the English Language* as informal.

Ambiguous wording

Ambiguity is a potential pitfall of all types of written communications and has already been discussed in Chapter 6. Although careful use of words can normally help to circumnavigate it, there are some obvious danger signals:

- *Vagueness*
  'most of the economies made'
  (Which economies were not made?)
  'some aspects were not discussed'
  (Which aspects were these?)
  'recently' 'shortly'
  (When?)
- *Euphemism and understatement*
  'not entirely satisfactory'
  (How unsatisfactory? In what ways was it so?)
  'causing concern'
  (In what ways? How seriously?)
- *Shortage of information*
  'for various reasons'
  (What reasons?)
  'disagreed...'
  (What were the reasons for disagreement?)
  'elsewhere...'
  (Where?)
  'possible problems'
  (What are these?)

Unnecessarily cumbersome phrases

Phrases such as the following may sound comforting but provide no useful information: 'having regard to the foregoing'; 'which they would be examining in due course' and 'in the light of the relevant circumstances'.

Malapropism and inaccuracy

During a meeting, people may misuse vocabulary through misunderstanding of the proper meaning of words. There is no point in reproducing poor usage; indeed, it can seem patronizing and rude to do so. The minute-author should also make sure that his/her own word choices are accurate. These minutes should have been corrected before distribution: 'There was a discrepancy among the members' (meaning disagreement); 'It was agreed that staff should be economic with parking-spaces' (meaning economical).

Changing gear

In speech, people will use colloquial and sometimes obscene vocabulary. None of this has any place in formal minutes. Just as there is a difference between formal and pompous styles of writing, so the sort of hyperbole and overstatement which sits comfortably in speech should be avoided in a minute record. For example, 'incredibly', 'literally', 'hopefully' (in its extended sense, meaning 'it is hoped that . . .') and 'fairly unique' (the extended sense of *unique* which is becoming widely used but is still resisted by traditionalists) may occur in the course of the meeting without giving rise to comment. When scrutinizing the written word, however, people will seize on their pet hates of idiom and take offence at words used in extended or dubious senses.

Example

This paragraph from minutes of the Management Committee of Tyne and Wear Passenger Transport Executive helps to illustrate the effect of individual words:

Current Holidays

P.T.E. Newcastle bus and engineering maintenance staffs were still
pressing for the introduction of current holiday entitlements and, as
a consequence of the County Council's refusal to consider this matter
until the time for next year's pay round, had withdrawn co-operation
in a number of key areas, including:-

  (i) refusal to operate into Wallsend bus station;

 (ii) refusal to operate special bus services during visit by
       Concorde;

(iii) refusal to implement a number of bus stop changes required;

 (iv) refusal to co-operate on matters related to Metro Phase V.

This item conveys a considerable amount of disagreement. While
the first sentence is uncomfortably long, the tenor of the discussion
is clear from the careful use of words. 'Still' shows that the discussion
has been raging over quite a long period. 'Refusal' indicates an
uncompromising attitude by the County Council, with little hope of
movement. The word 'key' shows that the obstacles are in vitally
important areas of operation. The repetition of the word 'refusal'
against each of the four numbered points is an oratorical device
favoured by political speakers: it works well here to give emphasis
to the intractability of the impasse.

Summary

Since every word means something slightly different, words should
be selected with suitable care. Deliberately chosen adverbs and adjectives
can do much to convey the tone and spirit of a meeting.

An up-to-date dictionary can give guidance on the respectability of
a word. A thesaurus can jog the memory in the search for a more
appropriate one.

8 MECHANICS

The ease with which the minutes are compiled depends directly on the chairman's handling of the meeting, the discipline imposed on contributors and adherence to the agenda. While in charge, chairmen must not inhibit discussion and freedom of expression. At the same time, they must not lose control of proceedings.

The chairmen should bear the following points in mind in ensuring their adequate control of the meeting. In this way they will greatly ease not only the deliberations of the meeting but also the compilation of the minutes.

- Is everyone getting a fair opportunity to contribute?
- Is anyone dominating the meeting unreasonably?
- Has comment been drawn from everyone with expert knowledge of the subject in question?
- Is enough time being left for the most important topics on the agenda?
- Is there any danger of the meeting as a whole running over time?

Chairmen will also ease their own jobs and those of the secretaries if they concentrate on maintaining the discipline of the meeting. They should:

- Define the limits of the discussion;
- Be impartial, but sometimes inject some pros and cons to ensure that the ground specified in the agenda is covered;
- Keep contributors to the point;
- Avoid arguing with individuals by throwing controversial points back to the larger membership.

Expertise in controlling garrulous discussion is difficult to acquire. Ten minutes was the average duration of an AGM chaired by Charles Clore; his biographers Clutterbuck and Devine described him as 'furious and resentful' when matters took longer.[1] However some excellent models of this kind of competence exist. Chief among them is Clement

Attlee, Prime Minister from 1945 to 1951: 'Thank you, Foreign Secretary, a most lucid explanation. Need you say more?' was his typically tactful way of silencing an over-zealous contributor.

Attlee was, ironically, helped by his grey and self-effacing personality (demonstrated by the contemporary joke: an empty taxi drew up and Mr Attlee got out). While chairmen must control a meeting they must never allow their personality nor – of course – their views to dominate the discussion. Many powerful and effective leaders have made poor chairmen.

For all his greyness, Attlee's handling of difficult meetings was brisk and efficient. Those attending his Cabinets found his summaries particularly succinct and impressive. This crispness made it extremely easy to minute his meetings. Equally it was easy to discern what action had to be taken and to take it. His own comments on the handling of opinions was particularly revealing:

> A Prime Minister has to know when to ask for an opinion. He can't always stop some Ministers offering theirs - you'll always have some people who'll talk on everything. But he can make sure to extract the opinions of those he wants when he needs them. The job of the Prime Minister is to get the general feeling - collect the voices. And then, when everything reasonable has been said, to get on with the job and say, 'Well, I think the decision of the Cabinet is this, that or the other. Any objections?' Usually there aren't.

Hugh Dalton recorded that a handful of Attlee's Cabinet lost their jobs - at least for a time - for talking too much in Cabinet.[2]

Some chairmen find it helpful to have in front of them a diagram of those present and to mark up every contribution they make.

```
     POPE
     111111

     HERRICK                          DRYDEN
     1

     GOLDSMITH                        SHAKESPEARE
     1111                             1

     SHERIDAN                         BACON
                                      11

                      CHAIR
```

The purpose of this somewhat laborious system is less to identify those who contribute excessively than to draw out the more backward participants.

Harold Macmillan required his Cabinet to sit round a lozenge-shaped table, so that Ministers farthest from him could hear, talk and see easily.[3] Eden favoured individual consultations with colleagues for lengthy periods rather than formal meetings. In this he imitated Baldwin, who made much use of this technique.[4]

Chairmen should, if possible, do their best to help the secretary as the meeting proceeds - for instance, by avoiding any departure from the agenda. Sometimes this is inescapable, as when an important contributor has to leave the meeting early, but should be minimized. More important, the chairman should give the minute-taker guidance in the balance and treatment of the account. Suggestions as to items of particular confidentiality, of special importance and those which should not be recorded will all be helpful to the secretary.

Especially useful will be occasional summaries of important points by the chairman. These take little time and do ensure that a properly balanced account is produced, with nothing important omitted. The secretary should not write such summaries down but take the opportunity to check that the half-dozen items so singled out by the chairman are represented in the rough notes and that justice has been done to them.

Some chairman feel the urge to redraft minutes or even to alter them unrecognizably. It is most unusual for Cabinet minutes to be changed: they are read to the relevant senior official and amended only if there is a problem of understanding. Sometimes it is necessary to alter the vocabulary or to add a neutral background. Crossman wrote of Harold Wilson's Cabinet minutes:

> When he was defeated he tried to pretend that he hadn't made the proposal and had the whole story removed from Cabinet minutes.[5]

Many chairman succeed in altering the balance of minutes without participants objecting. When those who have been present raise an objection, such alterations must not be made. Minor tinkering with the wording usually passes unheeded and is generally harmless.

Jokes, whether from a tactful chairman or from another participant, may have a very important part to play in breaking a deadlock or easing tension at a meeting. In the early 1960s the board of Legal & General were scrutinizing the profitability of their activities. At a particularly tense board meeting, the chairman, Lord Hardcourt, called urgently for figures to see how many of their shop properties showed a return over the magic 10 per cent. Those present felt certain that few, if any, would have done so. Arthur Green, who had been summoned to present the data, knew better and derived some small satisfaction from the occasion. He was able to astonish the somewhat apprehensive board ranged round the table with: 'Would you like me, sir, to start with those of our properties showing a return in excess of 25 per cent?' It would have impossible to do justice to the impact of this in minutes without seeming impertinent.[6] Regrettably, jokes have no place in minutes. However important they may seem at the time, either to keep the meeting running smoothly or to clarify content, it is unlikely that any minute will do justice to the wit without being disproportionately long-winded.

Possibly more anxiety is caused to minute-takers by the form of rough notes than by any other subject. In principle, it is desirable to write down as much of the proceedings as possible. Irrelevance can always be pruned out, whereas it is difficult or embarrassing to fill in any gaps in the notes which are noticed after the meeting has finished. A full account in rough also provides valuable ammunition for refuting criticism of the finished minutes.

All this is easier said than done. It is less of a problem if the minute-taker has learned one of the various forms of shorthand available. Shorthands based on special symbols usually take some time to master, but can produce speeds virtually double those of alphabetic systems. The best known and longest established are Pitman and Gregg. The former is based on symbols derived from a cartwheel and makes subtle but essential distinctions in stroke thickness. The latter's symbols are derived from an ellipse and it makes no such tricky distinctions. Newer but as efficient systems include Simplex (American) and Teeline which use letters of the alphabet.

Alphabetic systems, such as Speedwriting and Speedhand, can be mastered extremely quickly. They involve use of simplified versions of the letters of the alphabet plus a range of other characters. Mechanical shorthand equipment, such as those used in court, are not discussed here. They are a luxury seldom available in a commercial environment, probably more because of the time required to transcribe and edit a full account than of the cost of the instrument.

Adequate individual forms of notetaking can be developed to suit personal preferences and techniques. Some obvious symbols present themselves (£, $, @) as do easily recognizable abbreviations (NUM, BAA). An example of notes written in a personal shorthand follows:

NOTES	DRAFT OUTLINE INTERPRETATION
Trav exhib	There would be a travelling
Sept	exhibition; certainly in
Aug? (hols?)	September (maybe in August,
14 Days Lon	although the holiday period
Brist	posed a problem).
Bham	It would run for 14 days
Manch	visiting London, Bristol,
Edin	Birmingham, Manchester,

Newc (!!! 1986 !!!)	Edinburgh and (in spite of what took place there in 1986) even Newcastle.
Advertise all main media No TV £ Newspapers Sun 　　　　　　Mirror 　　　　　　Star 　　　　　　Mail Meals @ spec prices for VIPs + Press	Advertising would take place in all main media except TV (too costly). Space would be taken in the *Sun*, the *Daily Mirror*, the *Star* and the *Daily Mail* Meals would be offered at special prices for VIPs and Press. After discussion
Free?X ⟨JHS MENUS⟩	it was agreed they would not be free.
14/5 Some co-op with suppliers	JHS to produce menus by 14 May. Some cooperation has been arranged with suppliers.
⟨JHS LIST⟩	JHS to produce list as soon as possible.
Blue Peter?	The producer of 'Blue Peter' would be approached
Preliminary ad Budgets	PDR produced preliminary advertising budgets.
⟨PDR produced BUDGETS⟩	
Poss displays Various places in S Eng and Mids. Agric shows need early booking.	A variety of other possible displays were discussed, with special emphasis on S. England and Midlands. a. Agricultural shows called for early bookings.
town centres eg Oxford, Coventry Town halls to be approached Major exhibs probably £>	b. Town centre sites were useful. Town halls (Oxford and Coventry) would be approached for booking arrangements. c. Major exhibitions were probably too expensive.

The notations – based on common sense and received abbreviations – probably speak for themselves. However a few points deserve clarification. The ringed items indicate that a document has been produced at the meeting or is due to be produced later. The question mark against 'Blue Peter' indicates that the programme's involvement was discussed and eventually agreed. In fact the position of this would probably need adjusting to be nearer the earlier reference to television. The last part of the discussion, about possible displays, indicates notes made during a more rambling discussion. Here it has proved desirable to underline the main themes in the argument to give the summary some structure.

A form of minute action pad designed for the company secretary's department in a pharmaceuticals company offers a more sophisticated system for keeping notes. A sheet illustrated in Figure 8.1.

SECRETARY'S ACTION NOTE PAD

Meeting of . . . . Committee on . . . . . (date)

POINT	AGENDA ITEM	ACTION REQUIRED	BY WHOM
A			
B			
C			
D			
E			
F			
G			
H			
I			
J			

Figure 8.1 Action pad

The materials used for recording minutes are very much a matter of personal taste and comfort. Pencils tend to be clearer and less messy than most ballpoint pens. It is unlikely that a reasonable speed of notetaking can be achieved with a fountain pen. Even if the pen has been refilled immediately before the meeting, it is imprudent to take minutes in pen without a bottle of ink and, indeed, blotting paper to hand. With pencils a pencil-sharpener is essential, together with a supply of extra pencils for rapid changeover. H pencils are not easy for quick writing and make for difficult interpretation. B pencils will call for immoderately frequent sharpening. HB pencils are certainly the best. A red pencil for marginal markings (for example, uncertain detail or specifics to be inserted later) is also a good idea. Propelling pencils break too easily during urgent writing.

A4 paper is generally most suitable, being large enough to prevent the pages having to be turned too often. Lined sheets give discipline to hasty notes. A ruled or printed margin is useful when it comes to sorting the notes afterwards. Numbering the pages boldly with circled numbers before the meeting ensures that they are kept in order. A treasury tag through a hole at the top left-hand corner will achieve the same effect. Some people prefer to use A5 ringed notebooks. This, of course, ensures the correct sequence but the size of pad, while admirable for shorthand, tends to be rather small for longhand rough notes.

Two schools of thought exist as to how much detail should be included in rough notes. One suggests that everything reasonably possible should be written down, while the other calls for the secretary making judgements on what is important and producing a much abbreviated account. The appropriate course of action will depend on the minute-taker's expertise in the subject-matter. However, it is usually best to keep as full notes as possible - they can always be pruned and weeded afterwards. If a thin record is kept it is often difficult or embarrassing to have to make inquiries of participants to fill in gaps in information afterwards. Indeed, if the contributors have gone home to widely diverse locations, it may be impossible to chase up the necessary detail in time for inclusion in the minutes.

The secretary may make a judgement which suggests omitting some detail from the minutes and take the opportunity to have a rest or check existing notes. Typically, the chairman may then turn and say, 'Yes, that was a particularly important point: I trust you have got it down.' The chairman's and the secretary's views of what is important may differ significantly. Of course, the minute-taker must exercise some judgement on content, which is why a human being is taking the record rather than a tape-recorder. Nevertheless including more rather than less detail is almost always advisable.

A frequent complaint is that minute-takers are expected to take minutes *and* to participate in the meeting. The simple answer is that they should not be required to do so, but poor attendance sometimes makes this inevitable. The chairman must come to terms with the fact that the minutes are likely to be of a lower standard in such circumstances than if the secretary had no other responsibilities. The secretary can ensure that the most important points are covered by checking that the following questions are answered:

- What decision was reached?
- Were any serious disagreements registered?
  (a) By whom?
  (b) On what grounds?
- By what date does the next action have to be taken?
- By whom?
- Where?

This is clearly a rather restrictive approach to minutes as a whole but it can ensure that all the ground is covered if the secretary has to take a full and energetic part in the meeting.

Minutes must be written up as quickly as possible afterwards, so that the cryptic notes which seemed clear at the time are not misinterpreted. In particular, if a major holiday period is in the offing, the minutes should be written up before the break. If the chairman wishes to sign the minutes, he will normally wish to see a draft beforehand. Drafts should generally not be circulated to other participants since this practice could lead to excessive and probably totally unnecessary corrections.

A useful expedient routine in Bayer Pharmaceuticals for several years was for the minutes of monthly meetings to be circulated about ten days before the event, with an action column fully completed. Those responsible for taking action would then be required to write a note under their name in the action column indicating what they had done. This annotated form of the minutes was then typed up and circulated a few days before the next meeting. The system had the advantages of disciplining those responsible for taking action and saving time at the next meeting which would have been taken up by background explanation.

In some companies all relevant papers are circulated in accordance with a recognized timetable. The following routine is used in another pharmaceutical company:

TIMETABLE (Working days only)

Item	Day	Committee Responsibility
Submission of draft papers to Committee Secretary	– 8	Member
Submission of draft Agenda and papers to Committee Chairman & return to Comm Sec.	– 7	Secretary

Item	Day	Committee Responsibility
Approval of draft Agenda & papers	− 6	Chairman
Agenda & papers to Committee members	− 5	Secretary
Meeting day	0	
First draft of minutes to Committee Chairman	+ 3	Secretary
Approval of minutes by Chairman	+ 4	Chairman
Issue of minutes to members	+ 5	Secretary

Minutes should always bear the date on which they are signed, not the date of the meeting. This clarifies how much information was available when any after notes were added. For example notes can be added to the minutes after a meeting in the light of important information which has come to light subsequently, e.g in the minutes of the meeting of 12 September:

It was agreed that the Christmas Fair would be held in the assembly rooms at Barchester Town Hall on 18 December.'

After Note 'The assembly rooms were seriously damaged by fire on 16 September'.

Any system whereby all participants at a meeting have the opportunity to discuss and amend minutes is to be used sparingly. If such circulation is considered necessary this can be done in one of two ways:

- *Loose Control*, whereby the draft minutes are passed from one participant to another and then returned to the secretary.
- *Tight Control*, whereby the draft is passed from the secretary to each participant and then returned to the secretary.

In either case a proforma should be used to ensure that the draft passes around in a suitable time-frame. Such a form for *tight control* is shown in Figure 8.2. Passing round several draft copies of the minutes at the same time may cause considerable editorial problems for the Secretary. The result will be a large number of independently amended versions which will all have to be coordinated into one set of minutes acceptable to all concerned.

Sometimes, as with the British Institute of Management minutes shown in Figure 3.1, minutes will be given a security classification. This should only be used for matters of special sensitivity. Sometimes coloured paper is used for minutes, or parts of minutes, of limited sensitivity: for example, school governors may reproduce sections of the minutes on different coloured paper if they are not to be distributed to teacher-governors. If minutes are sensitive, some control must be exercised over their distribution and circulation. Copies should generally be numbered and a list kept of the people to whom they have been sent. It is also desirable to number the pages in such a way as to include the total number of pages involved: 1 of 3, 2 of 3, 3 of 3.

The secretary should keep the verbatim notes at least until the next meeting, if not the meeting after that. This makes it easier to refute comments from those who might choose to manipulate the minutes after the event. The secretary's version, if it consists of full notes, will probably have greater credibility than participants' more superficial accounts.

```
DRAFT MINUTES OF THE_____(title)

MEETING HELD ON_____(date)




To_____    return to me by    _____

To_____    return to me by    _____

To_____    return to me by    _____

To_____    return to me by    _____

To_____    return to me by    _____




                                          _____
                                          Secretary
                                          Ext:
                                          Room:
```

Figure 8.2 Circulation sheet (tight)

Summary

Strong, careful control of a meeting can ensure that minutes are more accurate. Summaries by a chairman during the course of a meeting can ease the secretary's job.

Secretaries should develop their own personal shorthand to ensure that as much information as possible is recorded. It is easier to thin it out afterwards than to recall information from memory.

In circulating draft sets of minutes for comment, a system should be involved for controlling the itinerary and timing for passing the draft. A proforma may be helpful for this purpose.

Notes and references

1. David Clutterbuck and Marion Devine, *Clore: The Man and his Millions*, London: Weidenfeld and Nicholson, 1987.
2. Kenneth Harris, *Attlee*, London: Weidenfeld and Nicolson, 1982, 403.
3. Alistair Horne, *Macmillan*, London: Macmillan, 1988, II, 160.
4. Anthony Eden, *Full Circle*, London: Cassell, 1960.
5. *The Crossman Diaries*, introduced and edited by Anthony Howard, London: Magnum Books, 1979, pp.124, 702.
6. Charles Gordon, *The Two Tycoons*, London: Hamish Hamilton, 1984, 59.

9 EXHIBITS AND ATTACHMENTS

Frequently the discussion at a meeting will be complemented by copious paperwork, some of which may have been circulated beforehand. There may be maps, plans and diagrams on display at the meeting; there may even be physical exhibits. Whatever their form, consideration of such material by the meeting is likely to be an important part of the deliberations. It will be difficult to do justice to the discussion unless the illustrations are incorporated into the minutes.

A list or table discussed at the meeting may also be attached in the interests of completeness. A British Institute of Management Foundation Board of Directors meeting was discussing the Institute's international role. A paper setting out details of membership was quite properly attached to the minutes (see box) and continued this for three

---

BIM INDIVIDUAL MEMBERSHIP OVERSEAS

The BIM Individual Membership at 30 September 1982 based on the CA
FILE Analysis – HAY 02 dated 15 October 1982
(Management Review & Digest circulation was as listed.)
(Management Today circulation listed also.)

PO AREA	COUNTRY	MEMBERS
F001	ABU DHABI	75
F002	AFGHANISTAN	1
F003	AJMAN	2
F006	ALGERIA	8
F010	ANTIGUA	6
F012	ARGENTINA	10
F013	AUSTRALIA	508
F014	AUSTRIA	9

tightly packed A4 pages. It is usually not advisable to insert such papers into the main body of the minutes. They should be referred to where appropriate and added on as an appendix. The following guidelines are useful:

- The attachment must be referred to at the relevant point.
- The type of document (map, table or diagram) should be indicated.
- It must be made clear whether the document was actually examined by the meeting, whether it has been subsequently amended or modified or whether even newly-compiled.

A sentence such as the following will normally suffice:

```
Copies of these Targets are attached to these minutes.
```

If there are several papers attached, it may be useful to give them a number or a letter and to list them in order at the end of the minutes.

The same principles apply to agenda (treated separately in Appendix I). However the concept is so significant that a useful illustration can be provided here from an agenda of the International Affairs Committee of The Chartered Association of Certified Accountants, where massive documents (in one case 48 pages long) are attached for consideration by members before a meeting:

```
ASSOCIATION BRANCHES OVERSEAS

The overseas relations Secretary's report, giving the results of a
survey of the Association's existing network of overseas branches and
suggesting possible improvements in the service provided by the
Association, is attached by pages 59-69.
```

The page numbers can be put in by pen if time is tight on compiling the dossier.

With all cross-references, it should be clear what the reader is going to find, as in an item from the same Institute:

```
The analysis of the questionnaires returned after the Level 2 and
Level 3 Study Schools, held in April at New College, Oxford and Stoke
Rochford Hall, Grantham, is attached on page 13.
```

The apparently lengthy statement of the contents of the attached pages is important. Only if the reader receives guidance as to the general contents of those papers will he know whether to read them or not.

Sometimes facsimiles of overhead projector transparencies are attached exactly as they were shown. As this usually involves rather crude reproductions of Letraset, it is probably preferable to have them retyped.

The cumbersome nature of these attachments is widely recognized and shortcuts are sometimes possible. For example, the following paragraphs recently appeared in a set of Northern Telecom minutes:

```
In an effort to cut down the amount of paper that is generated and
the amount of time spent by participants in preparation for these
meetings, I would like to change the format both of the meetings and
the minutes.

I propose that one chart showing the schedule and current status
should be shown at the meeting, together with one showing the current
budget information. Status information will be noted in the minutes,
together with any issues and concerns that are arising. In this way,
the written part of the minutes will be a little longer . . . but we
should be able to dispense with the enormous wad of charts that
accompanies each set.
```

Special problems arise with particular types of display, such as maps and plans. These may be entirely clear at the meeting when they are being nursed through the discussion by their sponsor. However in later perusal - and particularly for those who were not there - ambiguities and uncertainties may arise. Display items must therefore:

● Have a clear and lucid title (which indicates the relevance of the map or plan);
● Have a north-point (however obvious it may be to the author);
● Be of a suitable scale to demonstrate the point in question;
● ave an adequate key (where shading or other symbols are involved);
● Have sufficient reference points, if dealing with a large geographical area. A map of Greater London showing the spread of a company's branches is useless unless reference points are shown to which the branches may be related, such as Knightsbridge or Oxford Street.

Tabulations are frequently used for very detailed reference. Serial numbers for lines and letters for columns can ease this:

(a)	(b)	(c)	(d)	(e)
1				
2				
3				
4				
5				
6				
7				
8				

Appendices

If appendices are attached to a set of minutes:

- Each one must be given a number or a letter for cross-reference for example, Appendix A, Appendix 3). This can take a simple form:

```
STAFF MATTERS

(a) Position - See Appendix I
```

- Each must be mentioned somewhere within the text of the minutes.
- Their sequence must correspond to the order in which they are mentioned in the text.
- It is often helpful to include a list of them, with complete titles, at the end of the minutes.

Summary

When documents are attached to a set of minutes, they must be mentioned in the body of the text. Any modification to a document since the meeting - however slight - must be indicated.

Maps and plans should be carefully labelled with a title, a scale, a north-point, a key, etc.

A list of the documents attached at the end of the minutes may be helpful.

10 THE MINUTE-TAKER'S CHECKLIST

Heading

1. Does it show the subject?
2. Does it show the date?
3. Does it show the place?

List of attendance

4. Are all those present listed?
5. Are they listed in a deliberate order (usually alphabetical or by seniority)?
6. Is the chairman specified?
7. Is the secretary specified?
8. Are those participants who were not present for the whole meeting identified, along with the items for which they were absent?
9. Are apologies recorded?

Body of the minutes

10. Do the minutes show 'matters arising'?
11. Are 'matters arising' cross-referenced to the previous minutes?

12. Are all the items in the agenda represented by separate components in the minutes?
13. Does each item cover
    (a) Background?
    (b) Discussion?
    (c) Agreement?
    (d) Action?
14. Are comments attributed to particular contributors only where absolutely necessary?
15. Is every action matched by a note in the action column?
16. Is responsibility in the action column aimed at the appropriate level: company, department or individual?

Signature

17. Are the minutes signed?
18. Are they dated, as at the date of the signature?

Distribution

19. Is there a clear distribution list?
20. Have copy addressees been shown?

Appendices and exhibits

21. Are all appendices in the minutes?
22. Have all appendices and exhibits been given a letter or a number?
23. Have all been mentioned in the minutes?
24. Is it clear whether they were actually seen by the meeting or whether they have been added subsequently?

Style

25. Are there any unnecessary words?
26. Are any words used in misleading senses (particularly verbs describing the meeting's activities: 'discussed', 'covered', 'debated' and so on)?
27. Are the minutes written in complete grammatical sentences?
28. Are those sentences of moderate length?
29. Are the names of participants described consistently (for example, full name underlined, full name not underlined, job title, initials)?
30. Are paragraphs numbered consistently throughout?

Appendix I: The agenda

Agenda (originally a plural word, but now often treated as singular, so that more than one will be described as 'agendas') are complementary to minutes. They will sometimes serve the purpose of convening the meeting, stating its place, time and purpose. They will list the points to be covered and the order in which the chairman foresees tackling them. They may even give some indication of the pace at which the meeting is likely to proceed. They will often indicate a need for attendance by any unusual people, perhaps for a particular item, and will tell members of any special preparation they need to do. In other words agenda tell the participants what is going to happen and what they are required to do beforehand. To achieve this, items must be sufficiently detailed.

Agenda will generally start with a statement of the name of the committee and the date and time of the meeting (if these are not obvious from precedent or routine). The place may also be mentioned. A set of agenda from the Chartered Association of Certified Accountants starts thus:

STUDENT SERVICES COMMITTEE

11.00 a.m., Thursday 18th July 1985

AGENDA

1. MINUTES
   Minutes of the meeting of 23 May 1985, previously circulated.

2. APOLOGIES

A very basic but complete agenda is set out below:

The Centre for British Teachers Limited

9TH AREA SECRETARIES MEETING ON 26.4.81 AT 10.00 A.M.

AGENDA
* * * * * *
1. Collaboration - Norman Walker's Visits
2. Questionnaire on Syllabus Progress
3. Materials Projects
4. English Language Societies
5. Evaluation Committee Sitrep
6. Evaluation Committee - HYC
7. Other Points - HYC

24.4.81

The Centre is an educational establishment with contracts with the ministries of education of various countries. Their routines are well-established and a simple agenda like this would suffice.

Frequently there will be a need for more specific guidance, as in this example from a public transport organization:

```
             DEPARTMENT OF CIVIL ENGINEERING

          TRAINING CO-ORDINATION COMMITTEE

          MEETING TO BE HELD ON 1ST MAY 1986

     AT 09.30 HOURS IN ROOM 310, ASHFIELD HOUSE

                   A G E N D A

     1. Minutes of previous meeting - 29th August, 1985
     2. Report on pilot Management Training Seminar
                                - Effective Used Time
                                - Managing Meetings
     3. Progress reports - Supervisory Training
                         - Management Training
     4. Training for Supervision of Contractors - discussion
     5. Pre-retirement Seminar - date for next one - SMC
     6. Any other business
```

The subdivisions of items 2 and 3 are important to ensure that participants come prepared to discuss both types of training in each case. The initials 'SMC' indicate responsibility for item 5. Putting a proposed date on the agenda is often a good idea, as it enables people to consult diaries and other sources before the meeting. The notation 'discussion' at item 4 is useful. This prompts all those attending to come with some observations ready.

Sometimes the agenda will be accompanied by paperwork, but this will not always be necessary. An agenda item may be extended to provide the necessary background detail, as in the following (from The Chartered Association of Certified Accountants):

```
STATISTICS

Student registrations for the period 1st January to 31st May, were
3,156 (2,967 new registration, of which 1,262 were Home
registrations, 1,705 were Overseas registrations) compared to 2,939
(2,770 new registrations, of which 1,151 were Home registrations,
1,619 were Overseas registrations, plus 169 re-registrations) for the
same period last year. The end of June statistics will be reported at
the meeting.
```

Arguably the numerical data could have been tabulated.

Another example of a simple agenda is the following from Bayer Pharmaceuticals:

<u>Statistics/Clinical Research Meeting</u>

<u>Thursday, 5th March, at 10.00 am 2nd Floor Medical Meeting Room</u>

<u>AGENDA</u>

1. Development of Statistics Group.

2. Processing a Study.

3. Format and Content of Statistical Report.

4. Statistical Service/Needs.

5. Capacity of Statistics Group.

6. Links with AER Co-ordinator.

7. Future developments.

8. A.O.B.

Buffet lunch will be served at 12.30 pm

Copies J.Curram
        J. J. F. Herbert
        P. S. Leigh
        G. Macdonald
        H. Parker
        L. Porto
        J. A. Smart
        E. Streets
        R. Wheywell

Note the term 'A.O.B.' which, although colloquial, is a perfectly acceptable substitute for 'any other business' in internal minutes. Note also the timing of lunch, to give an indication of duration and an incentive for concise discussion. The list of people sent copies is useful – particularly for occasional *ad hoc* assemblies – to clarify who else has been summoned.

Sometimes even more guidance is required to enable the reader to do more specific preparation, as in the following document.

<u>TYNE AND WEAR PASSENGER TRANSPORT EXECUTIVE</u>

A Meeting of the Executive will be held in a
Boardroom, Cuthbert House, All Saints,
<u>on Tuesday, 14th September, 1982 at 10.00 a.m.</u>

<u>ITEM</u>	<u>AGENDA</u>	<u>INTRODUCED BY</u>
1.	To approve the Minutes of the 405th Meeting of the Executive held on 6th September, 1982 (attached).	CHAIRMAN
2.	To consider any matters arising from the previous Minutes.	CHAIRMAN
3.	To consider any Industrial Relations matters not otherwise included in the Agenda.	ADP
4.	To consider any Metro matters, including report on Metro Monitoring Study Before Survey Proposals (attached).	GMM/ADCLO
5.	To consider Manpower Budget.	APD
6.	To consider Platform Staff Establishment.	CHAIRMAN
7.	To consider Development of Fares Collection System.	CHAIRMAN
8.	To consider P.T.E. Office Accommodation.	CHAIRMAN
9.	To consider report on H.P.L. Management Training Programme (to follow).	ADP
10.	To consider report on Recommendations for Management Control (distributed)	CHAIRMAN
11.	To consider report on European Conference of Ministers of Transport (attached).	DE
12.	To consider report on Standby Arrangements - Storekeepers and Storemen (attached).	DE
13.	To consider any other agreed business.	

The opening 'To consider . . .' is appropriate here in this very formal
agenda but would seem out of place and repetitive in less structured

circumstances. The explanatory comments on distribution of the supporting reports are also worth noting.

With government or constitutional issues a formal style will again be fitting, with cross-references to files sometimes appropriate, as in this example from the States of Jersey:

```
10.  To receive a recommendation of the Controller that penalties for
     breakers of the Insular Insurance (Jersey) Law, 1950 should be
     increased (File No. 1/6).
```

Particular action may be indicated, as in the following:

```
Financial statement (Mr Keats to report on position as at 1.12.85).
```

Highly formal meetings may often call for the names of the anticipated proposer and seconder to appear in the agenda, in the interests of the smooth-running of the meeting, as in

```
The Chairman to ask for the
adoption of the Report to be moved.

PROPOSER: Mr A. Old
SECONDER: Mrs B. New
```

An idea of time allocation may be put against items which are of lesser importance but which could generate rambling discussion. This should simply be in the form:

```
10 minutes only
```

Any endeavour to tie items to particular periods, such as

```
12.10-12.20
```

is likely to be frustrated by earlier delays in the meeting. The specific timings will then be inaccurate, and attempts to control deliberations in this way will lose credibility.

Sub-headings in agenda are a useful way or organizing the sequence of discussion under a particular topic. This is particularly important with matters arising, as in the following example:

> 2. <u>Matters Arising</u>
>
> 2.1 Further Data
> 2.2 Retention of Information
> 2.3 List of Potential Users

In formal meetings, the agenda will often start with the minutes of the last meeting. This permits inaccuracies of detail and, more exceptionally, of emphasis to be identified. The last two items will probably be any other business and the date of the next meeting. A date should be proposed in the agenda for the next meeting, as:

> Date of Next Meeting (Monday 12 May suggested).

This enables participants to check commitments which would prevent them attending.

The numbers of the agenda items must be reflected in the minutes. If, for some perfectly good reason, an agenda item has not been discussed, the title must still appear, with explanation:

> Discussion on this item was postponed as up-to-date figures were not available.

For meetings which involve assembling a large and disparate attendance from far afield, it is often helpful to append a slip at the bottom of the agenda for those invited to return to the secretary, as shown below:

- -

Please complete and return to Personnel Department, as soon as possible.

* It is my intention to attend Site Committee on 9 June 1990.
* I shall be unable to attend and my deputy will be . . . .
* Delete as appropriate

Signed . . . .   Date . . . .

- -

It is usual and probably preferable to name an individual in the Personnel Department to whom to return the slip. A date for returning it is also more efficient than the generalized 'as soon as possible'.

The Video Arts film, 'Meetings, Bloody Meetings', contains a useful little section on agenda. There Timothy West, in the persona of the judge who guides the errant John Cleese through the various problematic meetings which are haunting his conscience, says: 'An agenda is not just a Chairman's crib-card. It is a brief for the whole meeting to work from.' It is probably the most important line in that excellent and deservedly successful film.

Even one-to-one meetings can benefit from a simple agenda. On being appointed Prime Minister, Harold Macmillan was disturbed to find his weekly audiences with the Queen stiff and unproductive. He therefore initiated a system whereby she was sent an agenda for these Tuesday meetings. This was immediately successful. It gave the Queen the opportunity to prepare her views and relevant questions, so that a more comfortable dialogue developed. The practice survives to this day.[1]

Sometimes, with matters of great moment, there will be a one-item agenda. Charles Gordon's memoir of Jack Cotton and Charles Clore describes such an agenda at a bizarre meeting on the occasion of Cotton's resignation:

> It was the most unusual board meeting held by City centre. It was like a scene from a Fellini film. Driving through the summer hush of a quiet weekday away from the hurly-burly of London to the soft green Thames valley, the directors and functionaries of City Centre Properties Limited were attending a board meeting to be held in the dining-room of the property magnate's country mansion. There was only one item on the agenda: the resignation of the Chairman.[2]

Sometimes a chairman's agenda will be prepared. This is drafted by the secretary to give advice to the chairman on how to handle each item. It is unlikely that it will be distributed further, although at large (or public) meetings, copies may be passed to others on the top table. This will include details of those who should be asked to speak, an indication of the importance of each item, the order in which they should be handled, any relevant timings subsequent to the meeting and any potential pitfalls. For example, under the title *Advertising 1991* might appear the following notes in a chairman's agenda:

```
5. Advertising 1991
   Plans must be finalized by 1 Aug
   J T speak first
   P L will press for more on TV
   Leave entertainment to last
   Cover:          Press
                   Hoardings
                   Calendars
```

```
          Freebies
          TV
          Entertainment

Problems with Herald 1988: several editions produced blurred copy
```

Notes and references

1. Alistair Horne, *Macmillan*, London: MacMillan, 1988, II, 169.
2. Charles Gordon, *The Two Tycoons* , London: Hamish Hamilton, 1984, (see ch. 8 p. 169).

Appendix II: Legal requirements

In the UK the various Companies Acts control the keeping of minutes of public companies. Detailed problems should, of course, be referred to a suitable legal adviser. However the following notes will serve to outline the principles involved.

Company general meetings

Every company must keep minutes of general meetings. These minutes, if signed by the chairman (either of that meeting or of the next meeting), are considered to be evidence of the proceedings, though not generally conclusive evidence. There is an exception to this general principle: the company articles can provide that minutes signed by the chairman shall be 'conclusive evidence without any further proof of the facts therein stated'. In these instances, evidence can only be called to contradict minutes if they have been fraudulently written up.

The chairman may make manuscript amendments which must be initialed, but nothing must be erased in any way as this would give rise to claims of falsification. Once the minutes have been signed, amendments may only be raised as matters arising.

Books containing minutes of general meetings must be available at the company's registered office and must be open to inspection by any member for at least two hours per day, without charge. Furthermore any member can demand a copy, and is entitled to receive this within seven days. The cost must not exceed 2.5 pence per 100 words. Courts can and have enforced this regulation. These minute books may be bound or loose-leaf (provided that precautions are taken against falsification). A company can now also hold its minutes on a computer.

Directors' meetings

Minutes of all proceedings of board minutes must be entered in the company's minute books. As with general meetings, these minutes must be signed by the chairman of that or the next meeting. They are then evidence of the proceedings. There is an assumption that any matter not mentioned was not raised. This may, of course, be rebutted by evidence to the contrary.

Statutory authority and textbooks

With regard to the Companies Act 1985, *The Company Lawyer, Guide to the 1985 Companies Act* provides an excellent source of reference. The most relevant sections of the 1985 Act are: s. 382: minutes; s. 383: inspection of minutes; s. 722: the form of minutes and precautions against falsification.

Other standard textbooks are listed in Appendix III.

Appendix III: Further reading

Chambers English Dictionary, Edinburgh, 1987.

Chambers Thesaurus, Edinburgh, 1987.

Collins English Dictionary, London, 1986.

The Company Lawyer Guide to the 1985 Companies Act, compiled by Ray Taylor, London, Longman Professional, 1985.

Concise Oxford Dictionary, 8th edn, Oxford, 1990.

Longman Dictionary of the English Language, Harlow, 1984.

C. Miller & K. Swift, *The Handbook of Non-Sexist Writing for Writers, Editors and Speakers*, 2nd British edn, revised and updated, London: The Women's Press, 1989.

M. Moore, *The Law and Procedure of Meetings*, London, Sweet & Maxwell, 1979.

Roget's Thesaurus London, Longman, 1987.

I. Shearman, *Shackleton on the Law and Practice of Meetings*, London, Sweet & Maxwell, 1983.

Index